TWAYNE'S WORLD AUTHORS SERIES
A Survey of the World's Literature

GERMANY

Ulrich Weisstein, Indiana University

EDITOR

Franz Grillparzer

TWAS 637

Franz Grillparzer

from an oil painting by Heinrich Hollpein, 1836

FRANZ GRILLPARZER

By BRUCE THOMPSON
University of Stirling, Scotland

TWAYNE PUBLISHERS
A DIVISION OF G.K. HALL & CO., BOSTON

Published in 1981 by Twayne Publishers,
A Division of G.K. Hall & Co.
All Rights Reserved

Printed on permanent/durable acid-free paper and bound
in the United States of America

First Printing

Library of Congress Cataloging in Publication Data

Thompson, Bruce.
Franz Grillparzer.

(Twayne's world authors series. Germany ; TWAS 637)
Bibliography: p. 156–61
Includes index.
1. Grillparzer, Franz, 1791–1872. 2. Authors,
Austrian—19th century—Biography. I. Series.
PT2265.T5   832′.6 [B]   81–4409
ISBN 0-8057-6481-X   AACR2

Contents

About the Author

The author was educated at Kettering Grammar School, North-amptonshire, England, and at University College London, graduating with First Class Honours in German in 1963. After a year at McMaster University, Canada, where he gained an M.A., he returned to England to lecture at Liverpool University. In 1971 he was awarded a Ph.D. by London University and at present lectures in German at Stirling University, Scotland. He is married, has two children, and lives in Dunblane, Perthshire. He has published books and articles on Grillparzer and related topics, and will shortly be publishing annotated editions of Grillparzer's *Ein Bruderzwist in Habsburg* and Brecht's *Der kaukasische Kreidekreis*.

Preface

This study is intended primarily for the nonspecialist, English-speaking reader, and aims to provide a general introduction to Grillparzer as a man and writer, and a critical guide for those who may be reading his works for the first time. Grillparzer is regarded as one of Austria's major writers, and has attracted considerable critical attention both in the German-speaking and English-speaking worlds, particularly since the last war. Because of the limitations imposed on it by length and scope, this study cannot enter· into a thorough discussion of all aspects of Grillparzer's life and works, which have been the subject of more specialized analysis. Nevertheless, an attempt is made here to indicate the more prominent features of his art, notably his exploitation of the visual side of drama, which has made him one of the most appealing dramatists in the German language; his subtle characterization; his masterly conception of challenging theatrical roles and his interest in the destructive aspects of sexuality, which stamp him as one of the foremost psychological writers of the nineteenth century; his skeptical and problematic treatment of ideals and institutions, and the generation, in his works, of a mood of fatality and ironic resignation, which betoken one of the supreme pessimists of the post-Classical age.

In providing a general introduction to Grillparzer's works in order of composition, the study aims to present a consistent point of view covering his entire work, relating it in particular both to the main events of his life and to his own Austrian cultural and political background. Grillparzer is a highly individualistic and "personal" writer, and the links between his life and art are strong. He also tends to occupy a somewhat isolated position on the cultural scene of his day, and for many years was regarded primarily as a latter-day Classicist writing in a Classical mode which had already outlived its time, and as a conservative figure defending outdated moral values and standards. Recently, however, he has been viewed increasingly as a more "modern" author who was contributing to developments in literature that found their fruition only after his death. In tune with these critical tendencies the present study stresses those aspects of his works that either link him with the more Realistic style of the late

nineteenth century or identify him as a more radical figure than that
suggested by the more traditional view of him.

Some of the material included in Chapter 5 appeared in "An
Off-stage Decision: An Examination of an Incident in Grillparzer's *Ein
Bruderzwist in Habsburg,*" *Forum for Modern Language Studies* 12
(1976): 137–48; and in "Grillparzer, Revolution and 1848," *Essays on
Grillparzer* (Hull, 1978), pp. 81–91. I am grateful to the General
Editors of these publications for permission to reprint. Some of my
conclusions are derived from observations recorded in an earlier
monograph, *A Sense of Irony: An Examination of the Tragedies of
Franz Grillparzer* (Frankfurt/M, 1976), parts of which also appeared
in *German Life and Letters,* NS 25 (1971–2), 210–19, and NS 30
(1976–7), 24–35, but there is no actual duplication of material between the previous study and the present one. Finally, I must record
my debt to my colleagues Dr. B. O. Murdoch and Dr. M. Read for
their encouragement and advice, and particularly to M. R. Mitchell
who permitted me to read his excellent unpublished analysis of *Die
Jüdin von Toledo.*

References to Grillparzer's writings and line references to his plays
are indicated in the text. In almost all cases the edition cited is the
readily available Hanser edition in four volumes, edited by Frank and
Pörnbacher. Occasionally reference is made to the standard critical
edition, edited by Sauer and Backmann, identified by the initials SB.
The collection of Grillparzer's conversations, edited by Sauer, is
identified by the initial G. Details of these items are provided under
Primary Sources in the bibliography.

BRUCE THOMPSON

University of Stirling, Scotland

Chronology

1837 Completed *Weh dem, der lügt!* (premiere 6 March 1838; publ. 1840).

1840 Completed Act II of *Esther* (remained a fragment; publ. 1863; premiere 29 March 1868). Founding member of the Concordia Society.

1841 Foundation of the Juridisch-politische Leseverein.

1842 Completed *Der arme Spielmann* (publ. 1847).

1843 Journey to Constantinople and Greece.

1845 Signatory to the petition on censorship.

1847 Founding member of the Akademie der Wissenschaften.

1848 Completed *Libussa* (publ. posthumously). Completed *Ein Bruderzwist in Habsburg* (revised 1849 and subsequently; publ. posthumously). 8 June: publication of "Feldmarschall Radetzky."

1851 Completed *Die Jüdin von Toledo* (publ. posthumously).

1861 Made a member of the Herrenhaus.

1864 Made a Freeman of Vienna.

1868 Voted in the Herrenhaus for the repeal of the Concordat.

1872 21 January: death.

CHAPTER 1

Life and Personality

I *The Background*

FRANZ Grillparzer's works are deeply rooted both in his personal life and in the life and atmosphere of the imperial city into which he was born. For centuries Vienna had been the city from which generations of Hapsburgs had ruled over their conglomeration of territories, to become known in Grillparzer's lifetime, in 1804, as the Austrian Empire. The eighty-one years of Grillparzer's life span an important period in Austrian history. In 1809 Vienna endured the humiliations of the occupation by Napoleon, while in Grillparzer's old age, in 1866, Austria suffered a catastrophic defeat at the hands of Prussia, and the empire had already begun its decline. During Grillparzer's main creative period, however, between 1815 and 1840, Austria, under Chancellor Metternich, was one of the most influential European powers. This period, which has since become known as the age of Biedermeier, was a time of economic expansion and prosperity, a comfortable middle-class age with an emphasis on cosy cheerfulness and material well-being. It was a time of pleasure-seeking, and travellers to Vienna drew a picture of gay crowds and sparkling festivities.[1]

But if there was a strong philistine tinge to Biedermeier Vienna, there was also considerable cultural activity, especially in music and drama. Private musical entertainments and song recitals were held regularly in the houses of the more affluent members of the bourgeoisie; the three popular suburban theaters and the two court theaters flourished in these years. For some time Grillparzer himself was a major figure on the cultural scene. His early plays enjoyed success at the Burgtheater. He associated frequently with other poets, and musicians too, for he met Beethoven, was acquainted with Schubert, who set several of his poems to music, and was a regular guest at musical gatherings in the 1820s. In his essay on the literary figures of the period, the dramatist Eduard von Bauernfeld describes

an intimate group of poets, actors, and artists who met regularly in
the Gasthaus zum Stern to discuss their ideas and projects.[2] He
mentions young men such as Nikolaus Lenau, Count Auersperg
("Anastasius Grün"), and Ferdinand Raimund, and refers particularly
to Grillparzer's wise and witty contributions.

This image of Viennese jollifications and of a witty, sociable, and
popular Grillparzer is, however, deceptive. Beneath the veneer of
charm and good humor there were serious grounds for dissatisfaction,
social and political tensions which were disturbing the contented
atmosphere of the city. Social unrest was due largely to the manner in
which Vienna and the empire were governed. The Emperor Francis I
and his chancellor Metternich clung obdurately to the outmoded
feudal traditions and absolutist principles of the Middle Ages, and
imposed upon Austria a harsh bureaucratic regime. With the bureau-
cracy went considerable restrictions on individual freedom, including censorship of literature, the theater, and the press. In Edward
Crankshaw's words, "the most perilous occupation in the days of
Metternich was intellectual exercise."[3] Austria was in effect an op-
pressive police state, and its intelligentsia and creative spirits suffered accordingly. The imperial family and the government seemed
out of touch with reformist developments in the rest of Europe, the
court itself was remote from most citizens and seemed to some to be
truly representative of an obviously decadent dynasty.[4] In this unsatisfactory situation, the pleasures of social life, music, and the
theater acted as a safety valve, and afforded the middle classes an
escape from reality. Crankshaw sums up the situation as follows:
"Since politics were forbidden ground, and since all ideas were
suspect, music, the theater, café-chatter, eating and drinking, dressing up, above all dancing, provided the only outlets for the surplus
energy of those who did not have to work sixteen hours a day to keep
body and soul together."[5] But not all spent their time in idle and
superficial pleasure-seeking. The winds of change were blowing
through Metternich's antiquated system, and a spirit of opposition
was developing among the more liberal-minded members of the
intelligentsia. Many of the conversations among Bauernfeld's circle in
the Stern were of a political nature, and the unofficial circulation of
satirical essays and poems was thriving. The crucial turning-point was
1830 when the July Revolution in Paris shook Metternich's system
considerably. The activities of the various opposition groups continued during the 1830s and 1840s until the outbreak of revolution in
Vienna in 1848.

Grillparzer's own position in relation to the political situation was problematic. For several reasons he was sympathetic to the liberal cause. Of middle-class origin, he had in his youth absorbed some of his father's enthusiasm for the enlightened principles of the Emperor Joseph II. He himself suffered during the 1820s from censorship and had several brushes with the authorities in Vienna. He also perceived that Metternich's policies were ultimately disadvantageous to Austria, and this offended his patriotic feelings. It was his patriotism, however, that led Grillparzer to disassociate himself from the more radical opposition groups. Throughout his life he remained loyal to the Hapsburg traditions and to the Hapsburg monarchy, and he was apprehensive lest the spread of liberalism should lead eventually to the breakup of the empire. Like many moderate liberals, he was also concerned that any shift in the political system toward democracy, republicanism, or popular sovereignty might let loose the forces of anarchy. Politically, then, Grillparzer was torn between his loyalty to the Hapsburg monarchy and his liberal principles. He was sensitive to the need for humanitarian reforms within the existing system, but fearful of what any fundamental alteration to the system might entail. Too politically conscious to participate mindlessly in the escapist and frivolous pleasure-seeking of many of his compatriots, he could not, however, sympathize wholeheartedly either with the conservative reactionaries of the regime or with the more radical liberals. During his middle years he occupied an increasingly lonely position on the fringe of politically minded circles, feeling more and more dissatisfied with the tendencies of his age.

II *Poet and Official*

Grillparzer's feelings of dissatisfaction were by no means limited to his assessment of the political situation in Austria. A résumé of his career as dramatist and civil servant reveals a series of disappointments which affected his state of mind and general attitude. "It saddens me," he wrote in 1849, "to think that everything that I have attempted in life has been a failure" (IV, 718). That this was an unjustifiable exaggeration goes without saying, but it is symptomatic of the mood of despondency that frequently overcame him as he reflected on the various misfortunes of his career.

Though Grillparzer came of a respectable middle-class family—his father was a lawyer—his boyhood was spent in gloomy circumstances amid considerable financial difficulties. Nevertheless, his interest in drama and poetry was fostered at an early age by the material available in the libraries of his father and of various relatives. He inherited his artistic talent from his mother, who was a member of the Sonnleithner family, and whose dominant passion was music. The Sonnleithners were a distinguished family, well-known for providing private cultural entertainment, and Grillparzer's uncle was, for a time, secretary to the Burgtheater. In 1809, while at the university, Grillparzer wrote his first tragedy, *Blanka von Kastilien*, but it provided his first disappointment, for it was rejected when he submitted it to the Burgtheater. There followed the years of financial difficulties after his father's death in 1809. To support his mother and brothers Grillparzer had to seek employment, first as a private tutor, then as an assistant in the court library, until in 1814 he commenced his full-time career in the civil service in the customs department. During this period his literary studies continued, and he also began to learn Spanish, even translating part of Calderón's *La vido es sueño* [Life is a Dream]. In 1816 the translation was published and brought with it an invitation to meet Josef Schreyvogel, the artistic director of the Burgtheater, who pressed the hesitant Grillparzer to discuss with him any current dramatic plans. Since the failure of *Blanka* Grillparzer had been totally lacking in self-confidence, and it required repeated encouragement from Schreyvogel before he could commence work on a new project. But then the whole play, entitled *Die Ahnfrau* [The Ancestress], was written within fifteen or sixteen days in a remarkably intense period of creative activity. It eventually enjoyed a successful premiere, and its reception, both in Vienna and in Germany, was sensational. Subsequently, however, supernatural elements in the play aroused fierce controversy, and it was attacked by Hebenstreit, the theater critic of the Vienna *Modenzeitung*, as an example of fate-tragedy. As a result, Grillparzer earned a degree of notoriety, and for years afterwards, when his more mature and more deserving plays were being disregarded by an unappreciative public, he continued to be well known in Vienna as "the author of *Die Ahnfrau.*"

Grillparzer was bitter at the attacks on his tragedy, which he felt had been misjudged, and looked for more simple material for his next work, which would be less open to misinterpretation. He found it in the story of the Greek poetess Sappho, and full of creative enthusiasm again, he completed his play within three weeks in the summer of 1817. *Sappho* was enthusiastically received, without any ensuing controversy, and Grillparzer began to reap the social and professional benefits of being a successful author. He frequented Caroline Pichler's famous salon, was on cordial terms with Schreyvogel, and was introduced to Metternich himself. He was also granted a regular salary by the Burgtheater, and he acquired in Count Stadion, the minister of finance, a powerful patron who persuaded Grillparzer's government department to grant him various privileges. But in 1819 came a turning point. On 23 January his mother committed suicide—she hanged herself in her bedroom—and it was Grillparzer who discovered her body. The shock of her death, in such ghastly circumstances, brought him to the verge of a nervous breakdown. Work on a new play, a treatment of the Medea legend, ceased, and the young poet was granted leave for reasons of ill health to travel to Italy.

Grillparzer's Italian journey is fully described in his diaries, and these illustrate how captivated he was by the architectural beauties of Florence, Venice, and Naples. But the real impact of the Italian experience is summed up in the poem "Campo Vaccino," inspired by the sight of the Roman Forum, which in Grillparzer's day was still overgrown with grass and used as pasture ground. It was indeed with Rome's decline that Grillparzer was concerned. He was struck by the ironic presence, among the ruins of ancient Rome, of a cross, the symbol of Christianity, erected by Pope Pius VII, and testifying to Rome's surrender to a new culture and civilization. His poem laments the passing of Rome's glories and casts an unfavorable light on the modern Christian city. On his return to Vienna the poem was published, but immediately gave offense, being taken for a thinly veiled attack on the Catholic Church and the person of the Pope himself. Grillparzer found himself once again at the center of controversy, but this time he was in trouble with the highest authorities. The emperor himself was angered, and Metternich initiated hasty measures against Grillparzer, who was reprimanded in person by Count Sedlnitzky, the chief of police. Now known as the poet who had had "that bother with the Pope," Grillparzer for years blamed the affair for his further difficulties with the censorship and failure to achieve professional advancement (IV, 109,642).

Promotion was indeed refused him several times during the early 1820s. He applied in vain for posts in other ministries, and for a position in the court library. At one time he considered resigning altogether, being convinced that there was a conspiracy against him to force him to do just that (IV, 642). It is easy to sympathize with Grillparzer, but it is also clear that he was scarcely a fully committed

worker. He overstepped his period of leave in Italy, and for the two
years following his return he was more often absent from his work
than present. He frequently applied for renewal of leave, and when
he was threatened with dismissal, his response was to request more
leave! In 1821 he had to be transferred to the finance ministry under
Count Stadion, so that he might be spared the hostility of his colleagues. In Grillparzer's defense it must be stressed that at this time
his greater interest by far was in his work for the theater, which he
regarded as something approaching a sacred duty, whereas his work
as an official was simply a burden and a necessary evil.

On his return from Italy Grillparzer resumed work on his adaptation of the Medea legend, and within a few months *Das goldene Vlieβ*
[The Golden Fleece] was complete, to receive its first performance in
1821. Unexpectedly, this was Grillparzer's first failure. It caused no
controversy, but generated no enthusiasm either, and financially it
was a disaster. As a result, Grillparzer began to lose confidence again.
New plays were planned and sketched but for a year he wrote little.
Then a new theme gripped him—the fate of Napoleon. When he was
struck by the similarity between Napoleon's career and that of King
Otakar II of Bohemia, he researched his material for nearly two years,
until in the winter of 1822–23 he at last commenced work on the play
itself. Remarkably, *König Ottokars Glück und Ende* [King Otakar's
Rise and Fall] took little more than a month to write. Eighteen
twenty-three was indeed a hopeful year, for in the summer
Grillparzer was promoted to the post of personal secretary to Count
Stadion. By the following winter, however, he was to suffer another
setback when, because of its depiction of conflicts between various
racial groups of the empire, and particularly because of its unsympathetic treatment of the Bohemians, his new tragedy was unexpectedly banned. Grillparzer was in despair and vowed never to write
again, but help came at length from an unexpected quarter. The
manuscript chanced to come into the hands of the empress, who was
impressed, and in February 1825 *König Ottokar* received its first
performance. Rumors that the play had at first been banned meant a
packed house, but the reception was mixed, and the Bohemians did
indeed take offense. Grillparzer even received threatening letters.

After this further disappointment Grillparzer went through
another period of despondency. The following year was largely un-
productive, for though he tried to work at various dramatic plans, and
completed a short story, *Das Kloster bei Sendomir* [The Monastery of
Sendomir], he had little enthusiasm for creative work. His troubles

were increased by a further brush with the authorities. This concerned his membership of the Ludlamshöhle, a club of artists and writers who used to meet in a local inn. Suspected of being politically subversive, it was raided by the police, Grillparzer's apartment was searched, and though innocent, he was interrogated and kept under house arrest for a day. At length, in the summer of 1826, he sought to put an end to his difficulties by undertaking a journey to Germany. Leave was duly granted, and his journey took him through Prague and Dresden to Berlin. The most noteworthy event, however, was his famous encounter with Goethe when he visited Weimar. Grillparzer was invited to a formal luncheon, and was so overwhelmed by the occasion that when the great man took his hand he burst into tears. Later during the visit he was invited to join Goethe for an evening's private discussion, but he could not pluck up the courage to go. The whole episode is illustrative of Grillparzer's lack of confidence in his own ability and in his stature as a writer. Nevertheless, his journey did have a beneficial effect. When he returned to Vienna, he began work on a new historical tragedy based on an incident in the reign of King Andreas II of Hungary. In a period of creative activity reminiscent of his earlier years, the first version was completed within two months. Moreover, because the play treated the theme of loyalty to the monarch, Grillparzer avoided trouble with censorship, and in February 1828 *Ein treuer Diener seines Herrn* [A Faithful Servant of his Master] was duly performed before an enthusiastic audience. The emperor himself expressed approval and showed a desire to acquire the manuscript for his own personal delectation. Yet Grillparzer, like all subsequent commentators, was quick to recognize in this gesture an attempt to suppress the play, which despite its "safe" theme also lauded Hungary at the expense of the Germans.

Now aged thirty-seven, Grillparzer should have been at the height of his creative powers. He was indeed already working on his next tragedy, a treatment of the Hero and Leander legend, but he had considerable difficulties with the later stages of the play, which was not performed until 1831, with the title *Des Meeres und der Liebe Wellen* [The Waves of the Sea and of Love]. By then, however, he was tackling other projects, and had completed *Der Traum ein Leben* [A Dream is Life], a play written in the tradition of the Viennese popular theater. The early 1830s were to be mixed years for Grillparzer. The failure of *Des Meeres und der Liebe Wellen* was partly alleviated by the complete success of *Der Traum ein Leben*, and professionally he received his long-awaited promotion, to the post of Archivdirektor (director to the court archive). But he showed little pleasure at this, looking upon the new responsibility as a further drag upon his dwindling poetic powers, and he was going through yet another sterile period.

These were the years of his friendship with Bauernfeld and the artists of the Stern, but in 1832 his great mentor Schreyvogel died, and for years afterwards Grillparzer felt isolated from theater circles in Vienna, who were paying more attention to a new rising star, Johann Nestroy. Eventually, in 1836, he sought relief, as he had ten years previously, in travel abroad. The journey of 1836 took him to Paris and London on a cultural and political pilgrimage. His chief preoccupations were the theater, the relatively liberal institutions of France and England, and visits to German radicals living abroad, such as Heinrich Heine and Ludwig Börne. Again travel appears to have had something of a therapeutic effect, for it was not long before he resumed work on his next play, the comedy *Weh dem, der lügt!* [Woe unto him who Lies].

Two disappointments were to await Grillparzer in 1838. First he was refused the post of superintendent of the university library, but more disastrous was the total failure of *Weh dem, der lügt!*, which was hooted and jeered by a cruelly unappreciative audience. The experience had a profound effect on Grillparzer. Though he continued to work on four major dramatic projects, three of which were completed—the exception was the fragment *Esther*—he withheld publication in his lifetime, and at one stage even gave instructions that the manuscripts should be destroyed after his death. During the 1840s Grillparzer withdrew more and more from social life, though it is wrong to assume that he led a completely isolated existence. These were the final years of the Vormärz (the "pre-March" or pre-revolutionary period), and Grillparzer remained in touch with liberal political circles. In 1840 he was a founding member of a society of artists called the Concordia; he became a member of the Juridisch-politische Leseverein (Legal and Political Reading Society), frequently attending its meetings; and in 1847 he was a founding member of the Akademie der Wissenschaften (Academy of Sciences). He also experienced a reawakening of his poetic powers. Of his final three great political tragedies, two, *Libussa* and *Ein Bruderzwist in Habsburg* [Fraternal Strife in Hapsburg], were complete by 1848, and *Die Jüdin von Toledo* [The Jewess of Toledo] was well under way. He also completed in 1847 his famous short story *Der arme Spielmann*

[The Poor Musician]. In 1843 he made another strenuous journey abroad, to Constantinople and Greece. His most critical experience in these years was undoubtedly the 1848 Revolution. Grillparzer welcomed its early stages in March, but when the radicals and extremists took charge of the revolution during the summer months, he felt alienated from their conduct and their aims. Twice during the year he had to seek security in the relative peace of Baden, in June when the publication of his poem "Feldmarschall Radetzky" aroused the hostility of the extremists, and in October when the revolution reached a peak of disorderliness and his own life was endangered.

The year 1848 marked the beginning of the last phase of Grillparzer's life, which despite earlier physical and mental ailments, was long and generally peaceful. Following his apparent change of colors during the revolution, he was in greater favor with the new regime, and after he retired from his post as Archivdirektor in 1856, he received various honors. In 1861, for example, he became a member of the Herrenhaus, the upper house of the Austrian parliament. Some of his plays were revived at the Burgtheater under the directorship of Heinrich Laube, but this belated success did not encourage any late flowering of his genius. After completing *Die Jüdin* in 1851, he wrote nothing more during the last twenty-one years of his life.

III   *The Artist and the Man*

That Grillparzer gradually ran out of inspiration is clear from a study of the genesis of his plays. The most productive and trouble-free period of his life lasted from 1816 to 1824, between his twenty-fifth and thirty-third years, and it was during these years that he conceived all his original ideas. All those plays that he completed were either begun or planned by 1824. Thereafter, he frequently abandoned projects, and he was often working on several at once, as he turned from one to the other in a painful search for inspiration. His last three tragedies, for example, occupied him over a period of some twenty-five years.

The decline in Grillparzer's creative powers, though gradual, was not however consistent, for there were clearly detectable "low" points, when his difficulties were especially acute. To some extent his problems were due to external factors. In his autobiography he refers to his professional disappointments, and in later years to financial difficulties and ill health, as inhibiting the creative process (IV, 115).

He was also wearied by his eternal battles with the "stupidity and evils" of the censorship (IV, 399), and discouraged by criticism and failure (IV, 111). Robbed of all self-confidence, he tended to brood over his problems, rather than to forget or sublimate them in creative activity (IV, 398). His greatest problem was his susceptibility to a state of mind that involved a blunting of his intellectual and emotional powers. As early as 1810 he wrote that his enthusiasm for life was dwindling, that he was indifferent to the fate of his new drama *Blanka von Kastilien*, even to pretty girls (IV, 251). In 1826 he had a similar experience, reporting on a feeling of dullness, of days devoid of thought and feeling. Nothing interested him, neither people nor pleasure, thoughts nor books (IV, 398). This time the indifference was accompanied by an inability to concentrate on a specific task or phenomenon, and he frequently complained of distractedness during this year (see, for example, IV, 401). Similar complaints are also found in his diary for 1821, and they were to reappear in 1831 and in the winter of 1833–34. At all these times his emptiness or distractedness was accompanied by a drying-up of his creative powers, and in 1833, for example, he lamented that the poet Grillparzer was dead, that whatever he attempted to produce in the way of poetry was stiff and cold (IV, 501). These periods of depression and sterility contrast markedly with those brief and rare spates of inspiration which enabled him to write some of his earlier plays at such great speed. Later, too, there were times when he forced himself to concentrate his thoughts and powers to the extent that he achieved that mental state of *Sammlung*, or "concentration" which he felt was necessary for the production of all great work (see IV, 389).[6] In such a state all external worries and distractions, all other interests even, were forgotten in the pursuit of one goal. Yet even when he did achieve this state he derived little pleasure from the creative act. For one thing he was too self-critical, as he reveals in his autobiography:

The peaceful joy of creation has been denied to me. I have always lived in my dreams and plans, but only with difficulty tried to put them into practice, because I knew that I would get no pleasure from this. The most unsparing self-criticism, which in earlier days I used to produce immediately after a work had been completed, I now [in the 1830s] began to voice during actual composition (IV, 162–3).

Art became for him a solemn duty, to which he felt obliged to apply his energies, but it was a painful duty, as he indicates in 1833: "It does not matter how much I suffer, it is simply necessary for something to be produced" (IV, 501).

The root cause of Grillparzer's psychological difficulties has been sought in his parental background.[7] His father was of a serious disposition, strict and withdrawn, an unattractive and ill-humored man, from whom Grillparzer may have inherited his own tendency toward despondency, self-inflicted isolation, and introspection. His mother was a far more spontaneous, out-going, and sociable person, but was sensitive, temperamental, even unbalanced. She suffered from hallucinations, was prone to moods of morbid despair and manic depression, which culminated eventually in her suicide. Her temperament left its mark on all four of her sons. The youngest, Adolf, himself committed suicide in 1817, Camillo suffered from hypochondria, and Karl lived for most of his life on the verge of insanity.

It was Grillparzer's greatest fear that he would go the same way as his mother and brothers. Certainly there is evidence that he inherited his mother's sensitivity and instability. He himself refers to the violence of his emotions, to his "sensitive and unstable temperament" (IV, 351), and to his "extremely excitable nervous system" (IV, 395)—quite the opposite state, it seems, from those periods of mental and emotional depression that robbed him of his vitality as a writer. Yet from his notes regarding the crisis of 1826 it is clear that the two conditions were not unconnected. After listing various matters which have been troubling him of late, he confesses that his whole life has been spent in a continual oscillation between overexcitement (*Überreiz*) and nervous exhaustion (*Abspannung*). The present paralysis of his sensitivities, he states, is a result of his overexertion of them earlier in the year (IV, 394). Previous crises also seem to have followed closely upon periods of intense nervous activity. Before complaining of his loss of interest in life in 1810, he writes: "For some time I have begun to notice that the violence of my emotions has ebbed considerably" (IV, 251), and in 1821 he contrasts his recent wealth of plans and ideas with his present poverty (IV, 362). Such diary entries certainly go some way toward explaining his periods of mental inertia and consequent creative problems, suggesting that he repeatedly drained himself of mental vitality and eventually burnt himself out.

The bouts of lethargy and distraction from which Grillparzer suffered are suggestive of a serious psychological condition involving intellectual and emotional inertia, a loss of interest in life and of contact with the world about him. The condition caused him considerable torment, and at least twice brought him to the brink of suicide. In 1810 he concludes: "In a word I am an unhappy man, and if fate does not remove me soon from this wretched situation, I shall put a bullet through my head" (IV, 251). In the same vein he writes in 1826:

"I see before me such a dark and empty abyss that I shudder, and the thought of killing myself has already occurred to me" (IV, 401). On both occasions it was his mental depression, not any specific external problem, which caused his suicidal despair. Grillparzer's symptoms of depression recurred in the 1830s, when a series of physical ailments and a sense of increasing old age added to his despondency and desire for death. In 1831, for example, he regretted not having been among those carried off by the cholera epidemic. Yet it is a striking fact that he lived for another forty years, displaying eventually a far greater mental and physical resilience than he himself would have thought possible. Bauernfeld's comments suggest that in these later years he drifted into a state of ironic resignation.[8] Bauernfeld, and Caroline Pichler too, were convinced that Grillparzer's main problem was hypochondria, that his anxiety over his health, both physical and mental, was obsessive and exaggerated.[9] Grillparzer may have drifted at times toward insanity and suicide, but his bouts of depression were never so severe that he put his suicidal threats into action, and he eventually learned to live with his mental problems as he moved into old age.[10]

IV   Social Life and Love

Although the foregoing account of Grillparzer's personality scarcely suggests an agreeable companion, his temperamental problems do not seem to have made him an unpopular man, or to have prevented him from winning either the sympathy or the love of others. He seems to have made a favorable personal impression, and even in 1826 was capable of entertaining the members of the Ludlamshöhle with his wit and gaiety (IV, 393,916). After their famous meeting, Goethe, making due allowance for Grillparzer's low spirits, reported that he was a pleasant and likeable man,[11] and although Heinrich Laube also had the misfortune to meet Grillparzer on one of his more despondent days in 1836, he found his tragic bearing deeply moving.[12]

The main friend of Grillparzer's youth was Georg Altmütter, a man full of generous good humor, who encouraged him in his poetic aspirations and gave him some confidence in his own abilities. In the early 1820s his confidant was the portrait painter Moritz Michael Daffinger, and from these years, too, date his association with the Fröhlich sisters, and his close friendship with the poet J. C. von Zedlitz and with Eduard von Bauernfeld, who himself profited considerably from years of collaboration with the older dramatist. The 1820s and early 1830s could scarcely have been years of loneliness, and Grillparzer was obviously highly regarded and sympathetically treated by his friends. Bauernfeld's own references to him are always generous, and in 1826 Grillparzer seems to have found a sympathetic audience in Beethoven, when he spoke of his unhappiness and his problems in the Gasthaus zur Eiche (IV, 916–9). Nor were his final years lived out in complete isolation. Summers were spent in Baden, and in Vienna he was looked after by the Fröhlich sisters, who were constantly on hand to attend to his various needs. There were also visits from admiring ladies such as Marie von Ebner-Eschenbach and Auguste von Littrow-Bischoff.

Nevertheless, there is evidence that Grillparzer's temperamental problems did overflow into his personal relationships. As a young man, he confesses to being a selfish and ungenerous friend, and to having behaved coldly toward Altmütter, for example (IV, 252–3). He reacted with bitter indignation when Daffinger became his rival for the love of Marie von Smolenitz, and he also quarreled with Zedlitz when the latter became a supporter of Metternich, and with Bauernfeld over their differences with regard to the 1848 Revolution. More significantly, he at one time describes his behavior as "gruff, cold, repellent, mocking, scornful" (IV, 433); he can disagree for disagreement's sake, however much this may hurt his companions (IV, 360); and in 1830 he confesses to an aversion to all people and to a desire to be left entirely alone (IV, 464–5). Yet Grillparzer was never able to shun human companionship altogether. However repulsive society appeared to him at times, his hypochondria in fact grew worse when he cut himself off (see especially IV, 458), and his need for friendship clearly communicated itself to those who were so willing to show him sympathy.

Into the latter category especially fall the various women in Grillparzer's life. For some commentators Grillparzer's love life has been the main object of interest, since it provided him with the source material for an important aspect of his work, his depiction of female characters. His relationship with Kathi Fröhlich, his "eternal fiancée", in particular, has become one of the most celebrated love affairs in the history of German literature. At the same time Grillparzer must be one of the most notorious bachelor authors, for a consistent feature of his relationships with members of the opposite sex was his own unwillingness to commit himself to any permanent attachment.

Grillparzer's first serious sexual involvement does not seem to have occurred until around the time of his mother's death, when he was twenty-eight, a fact which some commentators have found significant.[13] He then became involved with Charlotte, the wife of his cousin, Ferdinand von Paumgartten. The affair lasted three years, during which time Grillparzer was afflicted with pangs of guilt, mainly because Charlotte was more emotionally committed to the relationship than he was. The desire to disentangle himself was in part responsible for the Italian journey of 1819, but the liaison continued afterwards, apparently because Grillparzer found in her useful psychological material for the character of Medea. In 1827 Charlotte died, reproaching Grillparzer on her deathbed for being responsible for her state. Grillparzer was indifferent to her fate, but did feel disgusted at his own heartlessness, and recognized that he had emerged from the relationship with little credit (IV, 431–2). The profound effect that Grillparzer's personality could exert over women is revealed by the strange case of Marie von Piquot, whom Grillparzer had met in Caroline Pichler's salon. For a time, Grillparzer was an occasional guest of the Piquot family, but he ceased his visits when he suspected that he was being regarded as an attractive match for Marie. A year later, in 1822, Marie died, leaving in her will the information that she had harbored a secret passion for him, which had apparently brought about her death. Grillparzer received this information coldly, and suffered only brief regrets when he attended her funeral (IV, 191–5).

The main reason for Grillparzer's termination of his affair with Charlotte von Paumgartten was his engagement in March 1821 to Kathi, the youngest of the four Fröhlich sisters. The two had met at a musical evening only a few months previously, and that the engagement was indeed an over-hasty step is clear from the way in which the relationship developed. Quarrels quickly followed, some deliberately sought by Grillparzer in an attempt to annoy her (see IV, 363); some were of such violence that they had to be physically separated (IV, 477). Several times he tried to break formally with her, but amazingly they remained officially engaged for the rest of his life, and she displayed touching devotion to him during his old age. Grillparzer could not, however, commit himself to the marriage. Nor, it is generally assumed, did she ever become his mistress, not for reasons of morality, but because he did not wish to destroy the aesthetic pleasure afforded him by her purity.[14] His regard for her was too high for him to take this ultimate step, for experience had taught him that he quickly grew indifferent toward women with whom he had physical relations.

Not that Grillparzer was incapable of physical passion, as can be deduced from the manner of his infatuation for the beautiful Marie von Smolenitz, whom he met in 1823 when she was only fourteen. The affair was primarily of a sensual nature, for which Marie was as much to blame as Grillparzer himself.[15] But though she captivated him for a time more than any other woman, he became disillusioned, and intensely jealous when he discovered she had taken a new lover, his friend Daffinger. In 1826 he broke off the affair when she revealed that she was expecting a child by Daffinger. It was Marie who influenced his depictions of Erny in *Ein treuer Diener*, of Hero in *Des Meeres und der Liebe Wellen*, and of Rahel in *Die Jüdin*, all of whom reveal, in varying degrees, a latent sensuality underneath an apparent innocence. The extent of Grillparzer's passion for Marie might appear to belie his earlier protestation of 1821 that he was incapable of love (IV, 762). Indeed, when he looked back on the affair, he described the break with her in 1826 as a farewell to the last pleasant feeling of his life (IV, 489). Clearly his disillusionment was yet another major contributory factor to his psychological malaise of that year. In 1829, by which time she had become Daffinger's wife, his feelings were reawakened, and the affair was renewed. But they cooled again, and by 1832 she had a new lover, a situation which almost led to the breakup of her marriage, but in the face of which Grillparzer himself remained totally indifferent (IV, 489). It is ironic that he should have been so strongly attracted toward a woman as inconstant as Marie, and that he should have been unresponsive to others who were prepared to love him with more exclusive devotion. In the 1830s, for example, he had a close relationship with a girl half his age, Heloise Hoechner, who seems to have been a most unselfish and understanding companion. Yet he eventually avoided her, treated her coldly, and advised her to marry a Rumanian professor. Later, in 1843, as Frau von Continescu, she was bitterly disappointed that he did not visit her on his journey to Constantinople.

Grillparzer's failure to achieve lasting happiness in love has been attributed to his fanatical devotion to his art. Yet this could not have been the sole factor. His inability to commit himself to a permanent relationship, his occasional displays of callousness and cruelty, and his attitude toward sexual relations are symptoms of a psychological problem which was far more deeply rooted than a simple desire to pursue his work as a poet.

Grillparzer's love life represents yet another aspect of his life that was unsatisfactory. He suffered disappointments both as a writer and in his employment, endured varying degrees of inconvenience at the hands of the pre-1848 regime, and also became increasingly isolated from the various political factions of his day. As a poet he often became despondent when he could not find inspiration, yet he rarely got any pleasure from creative work when he did. As a friend he could be disagreeable and quarrelsome, yet he clearly needed companionship; as a lover he could be callous, hesitant, inconstant, yet he obviously appreciated the company of women, and on more than one occasion confessed to feeling the lack of a wife and family.[16] Grillparzer's moods of depression obviously derived from his disappointments, but they were also intensified by his own psychological makeup. They found their expression, in a variety of ways, in the tone and prevalent mood of his creative works, on which many of his experiences have left their mark.

CHAPTER 2

The Early Tragedies (1816–23)

I   Die Ahnfrau

FOR several reasons *Die Ahnfrau* [The Ancestress] represents, both in subject-matter and style, an unusual choice for Grillparzer to have made to mark his debut on the Viennese stage. For example, it bears little resemblance to *Blanka von Kastilien*, the tragedy of his youth which had been rejected by the Burgtheater, and which most commentators and editors have relegated to his juvenilia. *Blanka* was written in imitation of Schiller's early verse tragedy *Don Carlos*, the influence of which can be readily perceived in its elevated and occasionally verbose style, in its historical courtly setting, and in its universal theme of the conflict between duty and love. During the six years that passed after the rejection of *Blanka* Grillparzer read widely, particularly Goethe and Shakespeare, and he began his fruitful studies of Spanish drama. He also produced a vast number of notes for possible plays, and from the projects that got under way it is clear that he was still mainly interested in historical material. Yet in his discussion with Schreyvogel in 1816 he mentioned none of these projects, but instead a topic drawn from the world of the horror novel and the *Geisterstücke* ("ghost plays") of the Viennese popular theater. One reason for Grillparzer's radical change of direction may have been his realization that to be successful on the stage a play must have popular appeal.

In vogue at the time was a genre known as the fate-tragedy, which had been popularized by Zacharias Werner, Christian von Houwald, and Adolf Müllner. Their plays reflect the interest of the Romantics in the irrational and the supernatural, and their characters often appear doomed by some unseen power to commit crimes against those of their own blood. In that it presents the extinction of a family line in horrifyingly dramatic circumstances, involving the murder of the father by the son, an incestuous relationship between brother and sister, and a family ghost, Grillparzer's *Die Ahnfrau* appears to offer a typical example of this genre. The ghost is that of the ancestress of the Borotin family, who was killed by her husband for infidelity, and who, as legend has it, has been doomed to haunt the family until all her descendants are dead. When the play begins, it seems that only Count Borotin and his daughter Bertha are left, for his only son disappeared as a child and is believed to have drowned. Bertha has recently fallen in love with a stranger, Jaromir, who rescued her from robbers in the forest. Now Jaromir seeks sanctuary with them, having apparently himself been attacked by robbers. But his arrival is followed by that of soldiers, who have traced the robbers to the vicinity of Borotin's house. A battle, in which Borotin takes part, is fought between the robbers and the soldiers, and it is revealed that Jaromir is the leader of the robber-band. Worse still, Borotin is fatally wounded by Jaromir, and a captured robber discloses that Jaromir is none other than Borotin's long-lost son. Bertha subsequently dies of a broken heart, and Jaromir perishes in the embrace of the ghost of the ancestress.

In his efforts to achieve theatrical success Grillparzer resorts to the melodramatic devices typical of the fate-tragedy. For example, there is the fatal weapon, the dagger, with which the ancestress was murdered, which hangs ominously on the wall, and which Jaromir also uses to murder his father. The eerie atmosphere of the isolated Gothic hall and of the dark windy night outside also generates feelings of foreboding and terror. At times, too, the playwright descends to the level of popular comedy. For example, Jaromir places a handkerchief over his face so as to avoid being recognized by the soldiers, and the appearances of the ghostly figure spread confusion among the characters to the ghoulish delight of the audience. A significant influence on the play was Calderón, the seventeenth-century Spanish dramatist, whose *La vido es sueño* [Life is a Dream] Grillparzer had translated, and whose trochaic verse form he adopted. In places he does achieve the musicality of Calderón's language, often through the use of the kind of syntactical repetitions that the trochaic meter seems to inspire. A characteristic example is afforded by Borotin's envious description of the man fortunate enough to depart this life in the bosom of his family:

> Solches Scheiden heißt nicht Sterben;
> Denn er lebt im Angedenken,
> Lebt in seines Wirkens Früchten,
> Lebt in seiner Kinder Taten,
> Lebt in seiner Enkel Mund.   (65-9)

(Such a departure is not really a death, for he lives on in the memory, lives on in the fruits of his labors, lives on in the deeds of his children, in the stories of his grandchildren.)

Similar examples abound, with the result that many speeches have an effusive and declamatory quality. It was perhaps because of, rather than in spite of, these shortcomings that *Die Ahnfrau* was a sensational success, and the spectacle of the doomed family is reported to have sent a shudder of horror through Vienna. Nevertheless, the suggested presence of some supernatural power exercising a deterministic influence on the lives of the characters, causing them to sin as well as dooming them to destruction, was a concept that ran contrary to the prevailing intellectual currents of the time, and the critics who attacked the play as a fate-tragedy do appear to have had a good case.

Over the years, however, there have been many attempts to rescue the play from its stigma. It has been pointed out, for example, that there is no absolute proof that a fatal force is at work, but only a legend existing in the minds of the characters. Secondly, the ancestress herself can hardly be regarded as an emissary of fate, for her main function is to warn characters of approaching catastrophes. Her appearances represent an attempt to avert them, rather than to bring them about. Thirdly, the fatal force, if it exists at all, is given moral implications. It originates in a human sin, in the adultery of the ancestress, and her guilt seems to have been passed on to succeeding generations, an impression which is strengthened by her similarity in appearance to Bertha. Indeed the two are invariably played by the same actress. Thus *Die Ahnfrau* may be regarded as a tragedy of inherited guilt, and fate may be interpreted as an instrument of divine punishment.

But the aspect of the play that has received most attention is the character treatment. Later in life Grillparzer himself argued that the action would be entirely convincing even without the fatalistic elements (G IV, 1088), and it is true that events seem to result as much from the characters of those involved as from supernatural activity. Borotin's own fatalistic and negative attitude may be held responsible for his failure to dredge the pond after his son's disappearance, and for his pursuit of a lonely existence with his daughter, apparently cut off from all human society. This itself may help to explain Bertha's rapid and complete surrender to Jaromir's charms, and in her unquestioning love for him she exhibits something of the naiveté of the heroines of the Storm and Stress movement. The main motivating factor is the character of Jaromir. Brought up as a robber in ignorance of his noble lineage, he is totally unscrupulous in his attempts to gain a position in respectable society. He has clearly staged his "rescue" of Bertha in order to impress her; he deceives her and her father concerning his identity, and in particular tells Bertha a succession of lies over his role in the battle between the robbers and the forces of law and order. In several ways he is a forerunner of those reckless and egoistic adventurers whom Grillparzer was to treat in later plays.

These features of the play are certainly suggestive of a character-tragedy, of a tragedy of guilt with strong moral overtones. We are given the impression that fate is working itself out in the form of human passions, internal demonic forces which rob the characters of their reason and freedom of action.[1] In other words, Grillparzer, like Schiller before him in *Die Braut von Messina* [The Bride of Messina], has given us a more "modern," and psychologically acceptable, interpretation of fate than that offered in the fate-tragedies of many of his contemporaries.

But no interpretation of *Die Ahnfrau* can ignore the supernatural context within which the characters and events are portrayed. Although events are not predicted in detail, the legend in which the characters believe is substantiated by the dramatic outcome and visually by the appearances of the ghost. Whatever the moral justification for the downfall of the family, we are left with the impression that this has been contrived by a superior power of supernatural origin. The death of Jaromir in the ghost's embrace provides the final conclusive evidence. In *Die Ahnfrau* Grillparzer attempts to combine psychological motivation with fatalistic activity, presenting, for the benefit of the more sophisticated elements of his audience, the ingredients of character-tragedy within the context of an irrational and highly popular genre.

Regarding the question as to why Grillparzer should have chosen to dramatize a fatalistic theme in the first place, we return to our original assumption that his main purpose was to achieve theatrical success.[2] It is indeed the dramatic function of fate that Grillparzer stresses when he attempts to account for its presence in *Die Ahnfrau* (III, 310–11). In this connection the influence of Schreyvogel on the play is of considerable relevance.[3] Much has been made of Schreyvogel's alterations, but it is apparent that the bulk of his suggestions were concerned with making the play more effective dramatically. For example, he attempted to heighten dramatic tension by having the soldiers converse on the stage with Jaromir himself, without recognizing him. He also heightened the atmospheric power of the play with a speech full of fears and forebodings by Bertha at the conclusion of the second act. But his most striking innovations concerned the exploitation of Grillparzer's fatalistic material for dramatic purposes—in particular, Grillparzer's use of the ghost as a recurrent visual indication of the presence of fatalistic influence.[4] Its appearances on stage are used to produce immediately recognizable ironic effects. For example, its warnings of approaching disaster contrast markedly with the hopes expressed by Bertha for her marriage, and again with those of Jaromir, who assumes he will be purged of all guilt by marrying into this household. Throughout the play, the characters are confused by the similarity in appearance between the ghost and Bertha, often misinterpreting the warnings altogether, and we have Schreyvogel to thank for the appearance of the ghost at the moment when Jaromir takes the fatal dagger from the wall. This provides a vivid indication that the use of the dagger may be fatal to the family, but Jaromir actually welcomes the dagger as something which he recalls from the days of his childhood and, with words which have far more sinister implications than he realizes, he senses that fate is inviting him to take it. The young author who chose a fatalistic theme because he felt it would go down well in the theater did indeed profit greatly from his collaboration with Schreyvogel, and thereafter he was to attempt almost always to write with the theater audience in mind.

Grillparzer's dramatic exploitation of his fatalistic material combines with the various pessimistic utterances and gloomy predictions on the part of the characters, as well as with a considerable body of fatalistic imagery, to create a doom-ridden atmosphere[5] to which many critics have understandably been tempted to attribute some more generally symbolic significance. In particular, it has been regarded as an expression of Grillparzer's own fundamentally pessimistic outlook and as a reflection of his own unhappy circumstances at the time.[6] More generally, it has been interpreted as an expression of Romantic *Weltangst*,[7] as a representation of man's dependence on external powers and of his inability to shape his own destiny.[8] If viewed as an exercise in determinism, *Die Ahnfrau* may indeed be regarded as an anticipation of a far more realistic and rationally based view of the human situation which was to be popularized in the dramas of Naturalism later in the nineteenth century. However, Grillparzer himself adamantly denied any intention of representing a universal abstract idea (IV, 270). Apart from some fatalistic outpourings from Borotin and Jaromir, the tragedy contains few statements of

philosophical import, which would also suggest that in *Die Ahnfrau*
Grillparzer was more concerned with dramatic effects than with
thematic content.

II   Sappho

While the controversy over *Die Ahnfrau* was still raging in the
summer of 1817, Grillparzer was already at work on his next play,
which was to be a tragedy of a very different type. Deliberately
avoiding the sensational material of the fate-tragedy, he chose a topic
from the life of the Greek poetess Sappho, and in a conscious attempt
to recreate the atmosphere of Greek tragedy he achieved at times an
elegance and restraint scarcely to be expected from the author of *Die
Ahnfrau*.

Because of its formal and stylistic qualities *Sappho* appears to have
been written very much in the tradition of German Classicism as
exemplified in the verse dramas that Goethe and Schiller wrote
during their Weimar period. It is written in iambic blank verse, its
diction is stylized, and its tone elevated and dignified, so as to create a
more refined or heightened version of reality. There is an absence of
uncontrolled rhetoric, which characterized the longer speeches of
Die Ahnfrau, and structurally it possesses the kind of simplicity
associated with French Classical drama and found in Goethe's own
Iphigenie auf Tauris and *Torquato Tasso*, with a minimal number of
characters, a simple plot, and a strict observation of the unities of
time, place, and action.

The heroine is introduced as a successful poetess who returns in
triumph from Olympia to an enthusiastic welcome from her people.
Act I presents the announcement of her plan to seek domestic happiness through her union in love with the handsome Phaon, a young
man whom she has brought home with her from Olympia. But Phaon
is bewildered by her offer of love, regarding her more as an exalted
goddess than as a woman of flesh and blood. In Act II Sappho's failure
is already envisaged, when the preparations for the rose feast, which
she has planned in anticipation of her union with Phaon, serve only to
bring together Phaon and Melitta, one of her servant girls. By Act III
Sappho realizes that her hopes are dashed, and her jealousy is un-
leashed, to the extent that she threatens Melitta with a dagger. Then
in Act IV her jealousy turns to outrage, she attempts to banish
Melitta, and when Melitta and Phaon escape together by boat, an-

grily seeks revenge. In Act V, when the two lovers are brought back by force, Sappho's anger turns to shame, and she eventually throws herself down from a rock into the sea, to return to her true place with the gods. Thus the tragedy is given a symmetrical aspect by Sappho's attempt to regain the exalted image that she possessed at the beginning.

The language of *Sappho*, while restrained and occasionally refined, especially during Sappho's own long, reflective speeches, is scarcely lifeless. It is given expressive power by Grillparzer's frequent use of imagery, much of it drawn from the natural world of hills and valleys, woods and meadows, and the idyllic life of country people. Imagery is used to provide vivid illustration of particular situations. For example, when Sappho describes the poverty of a life devoted to art, she does so in terms of art "begging" from life, turning to Phaon with outstretched arms to provide a visual illustration of the point. Grillparzer's attention to visual detail is also seen in the rose which Melitta wears as visible evidence of Phaon's love for her. Joachim Kaiser, in his analysis of Grillparzer's dramatic style, stresses Grillparzer's symbolic use of objects, mentioning in particular his use in this play of the laurel wreath worn by the poetess, the lyre which she plays, the roses which she intends to use for her love feast, and the noble purple robes which she dons before her suicide.[9]

An element of realism is observable in the language spoken by the servant characters, and in this respect Grillparzer diverges significantly from the techniques of the German Classical drama. In particular, there are half-colloquialisms and short exclamations characteristic of real-life dialogue. "Why are you so angry with us, here we are, you see!" are Melitta's first words, while Rhamnes comments sarcastically on her naiveté with: "The girl does ask some silly questions!"

Grillparzer also departs from the regularity of the verse form by splitting lines between different speakers, particularly at moments of high drama. For example, as Melitta reaches up to pick a rose from a bush, she falls into Phaon's arms, and he kisses her. The dialogue is arranged as follows:

MELITTA. Ich falle!

PHAON.   Nein, ich halte dich!

der Zweig ist ihren Händen emporschnellend entschlüpft, sie taumelt und sinkt in Phaons Arme, die er ihr geöffnet entgegenhält

MELITTA.   O laß mich!

PHAON *sie an sich haltend.*
      Melitta!

MELITTA.   Weh mir, laß mich! Ach!

PHAON.   Melitta!

er drückt rasch einen Kuß auf ihre Lippen   (710f.)

(M: I'm falling! P: No, I'll hold you! *the branch has sprung up and slipped out of her hand, she tumbles and falls into Phaon's arms, which he holds out to catch her.* M: Oh, let me go! P: *holding her to himself.* Melitta! M: Oh dear, let me go! Oh! P: Melitta! *he quickly presses a kiss on to her lips.*)

Here the spectator will be unaware of the existence of verse form, as he concentrates on watching a sequence of dramatic action, whose effectiveness is enhanced when Sappho herself enters fortuitously at this moment.

    Grillparzer was first attracted to his material by Sappho's personality. He saw her as a creature of fierce passions, which she had controlled only with great difficulty, until they had broken out at a moment of crisis. It was this psychological crisis that he chose to dramatize, and in his revelation of Sappho's emotions he also shows signs of the Realist's approach. This is not to suggest that he makes no use of traditional Classical devices such as monologues and asides. In Act III Sappho expresses her disappointment over her failure in love in a long monologue, and it is in an aside that she first expresses her misgivings as she looks at Melitta. In this line, "Oh heavens, how beautiful she is!" (1019), she betrays her realization that she has been defeated. But Grillparzer also adds a stage direction to the effect that Sappho covers her face with her hands, thus capturing her emotions both in words and gesture. Sappho's feelings, this time of confusion, are also implied when she gives Melitta conflicting orders, first sending her away to dress, then ordering her to stay and be reprimanded: "Go and change your clothes! Off you go! Stop, where are you going? Stay here! Look at me!" (1088f.). Even a pause in the dialogue is sufficient to suggest her preoccupation after she has seen Phaon and Melitta kiss. Instead of discussing the incident, she pauses and simply says: "Phaon! You left our feast so early. You were missed!" (719f.). Grillparzer treats such moments of psychological drama very delicately, refusing to overstress them with long speeches of despair or anger. It is from such small beginnings that he eventually moves on to the moment of high drama when Sappho draws the dagger on

Melitta. If *Sappho* constituted Grillparzer's first unqualified success in the theater, it is to his credit that he achieved this not through the use of the kind of sensational devices that he employed in *Die Ahnfrau*, but through his subtle and skillful handling of his dramatic medium, in which he pays particular attention to visual elements and to characterization. Nowhere is this more apparent than in his depiction of the development of the love of Phaon and Melitta as something natural and innocent, in contrast to Sappho's conscious selection of Phaon for a specifically selfish purpose. Already Grillparzer was on the way toward the creation of his own characteristic dramatic style.

The main body of critical attention has not, however, been focused on *Sappho*'s dramatic qualities, but on Grillparzer's choice and handling of his main theme. Though he was to concentrate on analyzing Sappho's psychological problems, he also saw the opportunity of presenting them in terms of her position as an artist, and of exploring the general theme of the contrast between art and life. Consequently, *Sappho* has passed into the history of literature as Grillparzer's contribution to the long tradition of works treating the problem of the artist in society, and comparisons have been made particularly with its most obvious predecessor, Goethe's *Torquato Tasso*.

From the early stages of the play, Sappho's problems seem to be caused essentially by her role as artist. For all the fame and glory which she has won, her lofty calling has demanded of her considerable personal sacrifice. Her devotion to her art has meant a life of loneliness, and now with Phaon she hopes to make the crossing from the barren world of art to the golden land of love. But by Act III she has already achieved her insight into the tragic situation of the artist, with her realization that as a poetess she was not entitled to the happiness of an ordinary mortal. Once having chosen her calling she should have remained in the clouds with the gods, and not have ventured into the valleys of life:

> Von beiden Welten eine mußt du wählen,
> *Hast* du gewählt, dann ist kein Rücktritt mehr!   (952f.)

(Of these two worlds you must choose one, and once the choice is made, there is no return!)

Before her suicide Sappho again recognizes that the practice of her art has involved its necessary deprivations, and that she was not permitted to taste the joys of life to the full. In view of these sentiments it is tempting indeed to regard Sappho as a representative of all great artists, forced to live in splendid poetic isolation, detached from real life.[10]

But Grillparzer's interpretation of the artist's situation is more problematic. Moreover, it would also seem something of an over-simplification to attribute Sappho's suicide solely to the insight that she gains into her situation in Act III. It is at that point that the psychological interest in the play becomes dominant and Grillparzer's exploration of his theme more complex. Here too the serene atmosphere established early in the play by reflective speeches and by the elevated tone of the dialogue erupts into passion, violence, and intrigue with Sappho's outburst of jealous rage. The most crucial moment for an understanding of her suicide occurs at that point in Act V when Phaon expresses deep regret that Sappho in her jealousy and wickedness has destroyed the ideal image of perfection that he once worshipped. Now he begs her to reveal herself again as the goddess she was. And so Sappho takes the lyre and puts on the laurel wreath and purple robe, recapturing her former image, that of the poetess sacred to the gods. This, she feels, is her "true" image. But it is doubtful whether she will be able to sustain it, for her attempt to taste the joys of life has revealed to her her own weaknesses as an ordinary mortal, her jealous passions, even a potentiality for sin and crime. She feels that if she lives on she may well be tempted again to satisfy her human desires. She cannot live on and not "live." And if she suffers a similar reversal, she will again betray the image of perfection that people believe in. At the conclusion, then, Sappho cannot simply return to her art. Only through suicide can she pre-serve her identity as a divine creature.[11]

Sappho's suicide has been seen as an act of atonement for the betrayal of her art, as though she had offended some universal moral law associated with her calling.[12] She does indeed speak of her death as an atonement for the "final guilt of my life," though she does not specify precisely in what sense she is guilty. It is possible that she may be referring here to her original pursuit of Phaon's love, but her preoccupations in the later stages of the play suggest that she may be concerned about having betrayed her divine image. It is her death that affords her the only means of recapturing and sustaining this image. The play closes, as it began, with an assertion of the gulf between the artist and ordinary mortals, but while the former is still held by others to embody a superior and more perfect mode of existence, Sappho's experience suggests that it is a state that is virtually impossible to attain. It is her tragedy that she possesses ordinary human inclinations which prevent her from living up to the image of the artist which she and others cherish.

Though the image of the artist may be idealized in this play, the nature of the calling is not. Sappho feels that her life as an artist is empty and unfruitful. By contrast, the land of love, with its happy valleys, offers untold delights, and Phaon, endowed with life's most splendid qualities, is "beautiful," "noble," and "worthy." Naturally, after her disappointment, she says precisely the opposite, describing the realm of poetry in terms of flowers, eternal youth, cheerful meadows, and that of life in terms of poverty, treachery, crime, and a barren desert. Ultimately, then, Sappho finds herself faced with a dilemma. Devotion to her calling inevitably involves intolerable personal deprivations; but any attempt to satisfy her more human desires may mean disappointment, a release of sinful passions, and a consequent loss of reputation. Sappho is caught between two equally unattractive alternatives; neither art nor life holds out the prospect of complete happiness.

Grillparzer's view of the artist's dilemma is clearly an extreme and, one suspects, a highly personal one, and differs markedly from those of his predecessors. Goethe's sensitive poet Tasso has his own social problems, and also suffers rejection in love. As a result, he is brought to the brink of madness. But he eventually appears to come to terms with his situation and to be saved by his genius and by the value of his art. This is not the case with Sappho. Devotion to her art offers no such compensation. In the adulation of Sappho by the other characters there is something of the Romantic idealization of the artist as a superior, god-like creature, but we hear little, if anything, of the delights afforded by the adventures of the imagination, or of the ecstasies of the creative act. Sappho finds the demands of her calling too great, gains little happiness from it, is more aware of the disadvantages than the benefits. Grillparzer's artist is an incomplete person, her art is pursued at the expense of her more natural leanings. Viewed in this light, she is not so much a descendant of the Goethean or Romantic artist as a forerunner of the suffering outcasts of the early twentieth century, such as Thomas Mann's Tonio Kröger, who also learns the painful lesson that as an artist he cannot participate in a normal life, and Gustav von Aschenbach, who suffers a degrading and fatal release of passion after a life of discipline and self-control.

III   Das goldene Vließ

Following the success of *Sappho*, Grillparzer again sought inspiration in Greek legend, and embarked on an adaptation of the story of Medea. Once more it is the figure of a highly strung woman that holds the center of the stage, but in this respect *Das goldene Vließ* [The

Golden Fleece] marks a considerable advance over *Sappho*, for
Grillparzer was here faced with the problem of presenting a heroine
who is a genuine criminal, the murderess of her own children. In
addition, the relationship between Medea and her husband Jason is
analyzed in much greater psychological detail than the Sappho-Phaon
relationship, so much so that the *Vließ* has been regarded as one of
the first modern tragedies of marriage.[13]

Grillparzer decided at an early stage to present Medea's tragic
actions as the culmination of the story of the Golden Fleece, and it
was not long before he realized that this vast material would be best
embodied in a trilogy rather than in a single tragedy. In the first play,
Der Gastfreund [The Host], the Greek Phrixus has sought hospitality
in the barbaric land of Colchis; he is protected, as he thinks, by the
fleece of a golden ram, which has been offered to him by the god
Peronto. But Peronto is the god of Colchis, and the local king Aietes
regards Phrixus' possession of the fleece as theft. To avenge the god,
he treacherously murders him.

In this play Grillparzer has deliberately evoked an atmosphere of
primitive barbarism in order to illustrate the background of the
legend. Just as the servants in *Sappho* were characterized by their
occasional colloquialisms, so here the naiveté of the barbarians is
reflected in the simplicity of their language. Short lines and phrases,
an absence of sophisticated syntax, and a general tone of artlessness,
even uncouthness, characterize the following exchange between
Medea and her father Aietes:

AIETES.   Angekommen Männer
            Aus fernem Land,
            Bringen Gold, bringen Schätze,
            Reiche Beute.

MEDEA.   Wem?

AIETES.   Uns, wenn wir wollen.

MEDEA.   Uns?

AIETES.   's sind Fremde, sind Feinde,
            Kommen zu verwüsten unser Land.

MEDEA.   So geh hin und töte sie!

AIETES.   Zahlreich sind sie und stark bewehrt,
            Reich an List die fremden Männer,
            Leicht töten sie *uns*.

MEDEA.   So laß sie ziehn!   (97-108)

(A: Men, come from a distant land, bringing gold, bringing treasures, rich booty. M: For whom? A: For us, if we wish. M: For us? A: They're foreigners, enemies, come to lay waste our land. M: Go and kill them, then! A: There are many of them, and well armed, full of cunning, these foreigners, they might easily kill *us*. M: Then let them go.)

Again this is the approach of the Realist, and the episode as a whole, which possesses a distinctly satirical flavor, provides a further illustration of Grillparzer's occasional tendency to deviate from the elevated tone of the dramas of Weimar Classicism. The speech of the Colchians contrasts with the more elegant language of the sophisticated Greek, as also does Aietes's primitive trickery with Phrixus's more civilized approach. The emphasis is on action rather than reflection, whereas when we move on to Greece in the final play the opposite is true.

As Phrixus dies at the end of *Der Gastfreund*, he curses Aietes and calls on the god to avenge him. His call appears to be answered in the second play, *Die Argonauten* [The Argonauts], when Jason and his companions come to Colchis in pursuit of the fleece. Jason not only steals the fleece, but also carries off Medea, Aietes's daughter. Moreover, Aietes's son, Absyrtus, commits suicide when Jason attempts to take him hostage. But we are again given some indication that the sequence of catastrophes has not been halted. First Aietes curses Medea for her treachery, and prophesies her unhappiness as Jason's wife, and, then, as he dies, Absyrtus calls for further vengeance on Jason. Their words take us forward into the final play, *Medea*, to the heroine's savage murder of the innocent Kreusa, whom she sees as her rival for Jason's love, and finally to her destruction of her children. The characters seem inextricably caught up in a chain of revenge and requital which links together the events of the trilogy and generates an atmosphere of doom, which is reinforced by a series of curses, blood-curdling cries, horrific visions, calls for vengeance, and ominous prophecies such as those uttered by Medea to her father after the murder of Phrixus:

> Unglückselger, was hast du getan?
> Feuer geht aus von dir
> Und ergreift die Stützen deines Hauses,
> Das krachend einbricht
> Und uns begräbt.   (*Die Argonauten*, 113–7)

(Oh, you wretched man, what have you done? Fire is spreading from you, to devour the very pillars of your house, which will come crashing down and bury us all.)

At such moments we are back in the fatalistic world of *Die Ahnfrau*, and the use of fatalistic imagery, including images of fire, destruction, constriction, entrapment, and bondage, does indeed suggest the influence on events of some higher power.[14]

At times, the impression is given that this power is embodied in the fleece itself, the principal dramatic symbol of the trilogy, and that there is a causal link between the possession of the fleece and the ensuing disasters. Medea herself is convinced that it brings "calamity" and describes it as Phrixus's "fatal gift." The fleece is also given supernatural associations. It is hidden in a remote cave, guarded by a dragon, which threatens all who approach it with fire and poison. Later it is associated with Medea's magic arts, being placed in the chest whose contents bring death to Kreusa. But, significantly, there is no evidence that the fleece itself is an agent of doom, only a belief by individual characters that this is so. It has no death-bringing powers of its own, only by association, and these are in any case triggered by the characters. Grillparzer wanted the fleece to function simply as a symbol of ill-gotten gain (IV, 380), and its real powers are limited to its own dazzling and irresistible qualities. It appeals to Aietes's natural greed and to Jason's youthful ambition, and in this sense does indeed initiate a chain of fatal events. But these events represent the effects, not of some mysterious fateful power, but of ignoble human intentions. It is in their own hearts that the fates of the characters are to be found.

The two characters most fully drawn are Jason and Medea. In *Die Argonauten* Jason comes to Colchis as an adventurer in quest of the fleece, but his pursuit of Medea's love provides the main psychological interest. Jason's wooing of Medea is characterized by his aggression and violence, conveyed vividly by his behavior when he first breaks into her tower. Believing her to be some wild sorceress, he attacks her physically, wounding her in the arm. Then he suddenly seizes her hand and kisses her, rashly disregarding danger in the form of the approaching Colchians. The roughness of Jason's manner and the atmosphere of danger and excitement which is generated here provide striking evidence that in the interests of theatrical effect Grillparzer was prepared to relinquish the principles of dignity and restraint governing the German Classical tragedy.

Equally noteworthy is an absence of tender love scenes. Instead, in a series of brief encounters, Jason fights a running battle for Medea's love. He is attracted to her as to something strange and exotic which he wishes to conquer and possess, persuading her, coaxing her, almost commanding her to surrender to his wishes. Then, having induced her to confess her love for him, he loses no time in enlisting her support in his attempts to capture the fleece, and rides roughshod over her objections, finally carrying her off to Greece, away from her homeland.

But the true shallowness of his feelings is exposed in *Medea*. The omission of the intervening years emphasizes the contrast between the demanding, insistent figure of *Die Argonauten* and the callously indifferent husband. He greets her brusquely and then turns away, preoccupied with more important matters. When she attempts to please him by singing a song from his youth, he is harshly sarcastic. These are the outward symptoms of a marriage gone sour, and some of the longer exchanges between them have a Strindbergian quality in the terseness of the dialogue, the sharpness and bitterness of the tone, in the persistence of Medea's accusations, in Jason's unwillingness to admit error, and in the cruelty of some of his responses. For example, as Medea is about to go into exile, the following exchange takes place:

MEDEA.   Jason!

JASON.   *umkehrend.*
                  Was ist?

MEDEA.   Es ist das letztemal:
              Das letztemal vielleicht, daß wir uns sprechen!

JASON.   So laß uns scheiden ohne Haß und Groll.

MEDEA.   Du hast zu Liebe mich verlockt und fliehst mich?

JASON.   Ich muß.

MEDEA.   Du hast den Vater mir geraubt
              Und raubst mir den Gemahl?

JASON.   Gezwungen nur.

MEDEA.   Mein Bruder fiel durch dich, du nahmst mir ihn,
              Und fliehst mich?

JASON.   Wie er fiel, gleich unverschuldet.

MEDEA.   Mein Vaterland verließ ich, dir zu folgen.

JASON.   Dem eignen Willen folgtest du, nicht mir.
              Hätts dich gereut, gern ließ ich dich zurück!

MEDEA.   Die Welt verflucht um deinetwillen mich,
         Ich selber hasse mich um deinetwillen.
         Und du verläßt mich?

JASON.   Ich verlaß dich nicht,
         Ein höhrer Spruch treibt mich von dir hinweg.   (1556-70)

(M: Jason! J: *turning*. What is it? M: This is the last time, perhaps the very last
time that we shall see each other! J: Then let us part without hatred or
bitterness. M: You once seduced me into loving you, and now you shun me? J:
I must. M: You robbed me of my father, and now rob me of my husband? J:
Only because I am forced to. M: It was because of you that my brother fell,
you took him from me, and now you shun me? J: As free from blame as when
he fell. M: I left my homeland to follow you. J: You followed your own free
will, not me. If you had regretted it, I would gladly have left you behind! M:
For your sake the world curses me, for your sake I hate myself, and yet you
desert me? J: I am not deserting you. A higher judgment is driving me away
from you.)

Admittedly Jason has cause to be dissatisfied. His attempt to introduce the barbarian princess into civilized Greek society has failed.
His reception has been hostile, and people recoil in horror from her.
She has also been implicated in the murder of his uncle. Initially,
then, the tragedy depends on the incompatibility between barbarism
and Greek civilization, but ultimately the major factor in the failure of
the marriage is the attitude and character of Jason himself. Jason
shows no inclination at all to share Medea's fate, but is prepared to get
rid of her in order to save his own reputation and future happiness.
Bitterly Medea accuses him of seeking her love as an adventurer
seeks fame and fortune, of brutally playing with her feelings for his
own self-gratification, until casting her aside. Jason is one of
Grillparzer's selfish and ambitious heroes, a descendant of Jaromir in
Die Ahnfrau. Not that he is a truly villainous man, for Kreusa describes a different Jason of the past, a milder and more prepossessing
man. But he has been tempted by the lure of adventure, and he learns
the bitter lesson of the futility of ambition, ending as a broken man, a
singularly unheroic figure, bemoaning the glorious morning which
has turned into the blackness of night.
   But if Jason bears the major responsibility for the breakdown of the
marriage, Medea is by far the more striking figure. She is the first of
several female characters in whom Grillparzer has explored the onset
of passion, but the bitterness that she displays following Jason's
betrayal of her is unique in his tragedies. If Grillparzer was drawing

on his personal experiences with Charlotte von Paumgartten, then the Jason-Medea relationship is indeed a revealing piece of *Erlebnisdichtung*.

In *Die Argonauten* Grillparzer depicts Medea essentially as the defenseless victim of Jason's aggression, for she experiences love as an irresistible, bewildering force which takes over her being. Initially she attempts to resist it, regarding Jason as her enemy, suppressing her emotions, refusing to discuss the implications of their initial encounter, enthusiastically cooperating in her father's plans to drive the Greeks from their country. Several spontaneous actions are, however, sufficiently transparent to reveal a growing passion underneath her apparent hostility. At their first encounter she prevents her brother from attacking Jason, at the second she warns Jason that his drink is poisoned. She feels that Jason has kindled a fire within her, with the sparks which emanate from his being. Here the demonic power of love and sexual attraction is represented in a most dangerous form. The image of fire is to recur frequently, in the flames of the venomous dragon which guards the fleece, in the dazzling properties of the fleece itself, and in Medea's own magic arts, which are to consume Kreon's palace in flames. Through the imagery of the trilogy these phenomena become a poetic extension of Medea's passions.[15]

But only in *Medea* do the heroine's passions in themselves become dangerous, when her jealousy is aroused and her love turns to hatred—and this only because of the way the situation has developed and because of Jason's reaction. Grillparzer is clearly intent on presenting Medea as a victim of circumstances rather than as an inherently wicked woman. Her attitude toward the situation is favorably contrasted with Jason's attitude. As *Medea* opens she is seen burying the fleece, attempting to put the past behind her and even to make the marriage work, and on Jason's terms, too, for she is prepared to renounce her barbaric origins and adopt the trappings of Greek civilization. But underneath she is full of resentment, and her hatred begins to show through. Grillparzer captures the nature of her emotions in a striking piece of drama, which occurs when Jason pours scorn on her attempts to play the lyre. As he tries to take the lyre from her, she breaks it into pieces, exulting at this release of her pent-up feelings. With this incident Grillparzer is also beginning his careful delineation of the motivation of her crimes. Medea's bitterness increases when Jason refuses to share her banishment and shows renewed interest in his childhood sweetheart, the Princess Kreusa. But at the end of Act III Medea's feelings come to a head. In response to her appeal that she might take her children with her into exile, Jason agrees that one of them shall accompany her, though on a voluntary basis. But when the choice is put to the children, they both refuse, seeking protection instead with the gentle Kreusa. Medea feels rejected, is filled with a fierce desire for vengeance against one and all. But ultimately the murders are the results of sudden impulses. The decision to kill Kreusa is taken hastily, when Kreon, in his attempt to wrest the fleece from her, suggests that she should send it to Kreusa in its chest. Joyfully she seizes on this opportunity, for she knows the chest conceals her fatal fires. Thereafter, she kills her children, not in a fit of rage, but when she realizes that they may well suffer as a result of her murder of Kreusa. Grillparzer demonstrates that she is pushed to extreme lengths, acting irrationally under pressure rather than with premeditated villainy. It is appropriate that for the murder of Kreusa, Medea should resurrect the fleece and employ her old magic arts. In so doing, she assumes her old identity and returns to her barbaric roots, and the trilogy comes full circle as she indulges in an orgy of primitive vengeance.

Following the savagery of Medea's behavior, it is also fitting that the final scene of *Medea* should have a wild and remote setting, which, with its forests and rocks, is almost identical to the setting used for the opening of the trilogy. Here Jason and Medea encounter each other for the last time, and one might reasonably expect that the chain of vengenace will continue. Jason does indeed reach for his sword to slay Medea, but she stops him with a word. She feels that neither death at the hands of Jason nor indeed suicide would constitute an adequate punishment. While Jason can only bemoan the fate of the children and long for death, Medea conceives of a punishment that is more dire than death, namely, to live on in the knowledge of her crimes. Death would simply amount to an escape from her wretchedness. Instead, Medea, like the Oedipus of Sophocles, will wander the world bearing the pain of her guilt, and will eventually submit herself to the judgment of Apollo. Clearly Grillparzer is bent on giving Medea some stature as a heroine, her strength of character being contrasted to the weakness of the now-broken Jason. She also reminds him of his role in the sequence of tragic events in famous lines denoting the futility of the pursuit of happiness and fame:

> Was ist der Erde Glück?—Ein Schatten!
> Was ist der Erde Ruhm?—Ein Traum!
> Du Armer! der von Schatten du geträumt!
> Der Traum ist aus, allein die Nacht noch nicht. (2366–9)

(What is earthly happiness?—A shadow! What is earthly fame?—A dream!
You poor man, who dreamt of shadows! The dream is over, but not yet the
night.)

For all his veneer of civilization, Jason must bear his share of the guilt
for what has come to pass. Some have seen in Medea's attitude an
attempt on Grillparzer's part to endow her with a moral superiority
over the unfortunate Jason.[16] But while accusing Jason, she is in no
way attempting to detract from her own guilt. Indeed, by deliberately
prolonging her agony and suggesting that only a superior being may
judge her, she is only underlining her awareness of sin. Though she
achieves in her final speech a remarkable calmness, this is not due to
any sense of moral superiority or triumph. Here, in the words of T. C.
Dunham, it is a matter of "all passion spent, but with no peace of
mind."[17] Both the civilized Greek and the barbarian princess are
guilty in their different ways, so that the original contrast between
barbarism and civilization is both superficial and misleading, and is
eventually transcended. The trilogy provides a sorry record of human
fallibility, and ends fittingly in an atmosphere of resignation, with an
honest appraisal of guilt and a willingness to atone. Nor is the mood
alleviated by any act of atonement. The spiritual anguish of Jason and
Medea continues beyond the conclusion of this most pessimistic of
Grillparzer's early tragedies.

IV   König Ottokars Glück und Ende

Grillparzer's interest in Greek legend did not diminish after he had
completed *Das goldene Vlieβ*, and while rehearsals were going ahead
for the premiere in the winter of 1820–21, he was already planning an
adaptation of the story of Hero and Leander. But, following the
somewhat modest success of his trilogy, he abandoned his new project and, spurred on by his interest in Napoleon and his discovery of
an historical parallel, he returned to a genre that had attracted him in
the early years, the historical tragedy. Grillparzer himself felt that
König Ottokars Glück und Ende [King Otakar's Rise and Fall] was his
finest play. It encompasses over twenty years of history, is written on
the grand scale, in the spirit of Shakespeare's historical pageants, with
a large array of characters and spectacular scenes, and has been
praised above all for its theatrical qualities; for the opportunities
which it affords for fine acting; for its vivid scenes of confrontation and
for the visual qualities of the stage action; for its expressive, flexible
language, use of eloquent objects and gestures; for its skillful stage

arrangements, colorful settings and costumes; all of which for Walter Silz show "the master of theater who completely visualized his work."[18] At last, it seemed, Grillparzer had succeeded in investing a serious tragic subject with popular dramatic appeal. A significant factor was Grillparzer's exploitation of the historical coincidence of Otakar's downfall with the election in 1273 of the first Hapsburg, Rudolph I, as Holy Roman Emperor, and the foundation of the Hapsburg dynasty in Austria. This was a golden opportunity for an Austrian dramatist to introduce a patriotic theme into the play, so Grillparzer idealized Rudolph, bestowing upon him the qualities of the model ruler. Grillparzer's concurrence with the actor Heurteur that the latter should play the role of Rudolf "half like Emperor Francis and half like Saint Florian" (IV, 126) might even indicate that he intended the figure of Rudolf as a tribute to his own emperor. But in view of his experiences following the publication in 1819 of his poem "Campo Vaccino," and his opinions generally of the Metternich regime, it is more likely that he invested Rudolf with qualities that the ruler of his own day did not himself possess, but which he felt had been possessed by Joseph II, who died in the year before Grillparzer was born. In so doing he may have been attempting to put an attractive and misleading gloss over the more serious and potentially dangerous political aspects of the play.

The pivot of the action is the election of Rudolf as emperor instead of Ottokar, and the main issue of conflict is provided by the ensuing dispute between the two over the territories of Austria and Styria, which Ottokar had gained through marriage to Margarethe of Austria. Initially, Ottokar is seen at the height of his power, flushed by recent success in battle, and during the first act he acquires still more lands. When the emissaries arrive from Frankfurt, where the electors have assembled to choose a new emperor, he reaches his zenith, and his people already hail him as emperor. In this first act, however, Ottokar has already made the mistake that will ultimately lead to his downfall. This is his decision to divorce his wife, Margarethe, to marry Kunigunde, niece of the King of Hungary, a decision precipitated in part by Ottokar's desire for an heir, which Margarethe is too old to provide. But Margarethe herself rejects Ottokar's trumped-up reasons for the divorce, which she regards as an immoral act, as the severance of a sacred bond. Subsequently, complaints are made against him to the electors, who duly turn to Rudolf as someone who is Ottokar's moral superior. By the end of Act II the moral issue has turned into a legal conflict between Ottokar and the new emperor, who has demanded that Ottokar return to the Reich those lands that he had gained when he married Margarethe. The result is a military conflict. There are no actual battle scenes, but two long scenes in their respective camps tell us that Rudolf is in the ascendancy and has already asserted his moral authority over the empire as a whole. When, therefore, Ottokar is persuaded to attend a peace conference near Vienna, he has to surrender the disputed territories and recognize Rudolf's authority. The third act thus ends with Ottokar's submission and the promise of an era of peaceful cooperation. That this is a false climax is revealed in Act IV, when Ottokar returns home from his humiliation. Instead of complying with fresh demands from Rudolf that he surrender hostages which he had taken prior to the conflict, he is goaded into defying Rudolf again, with fatal results in Act V.

The structure of this tragedy encourages a moral interpretation of Ottokar's career, according to which Ottokar is taught a lesson relating both to his defiance of the law and to his conduct generally as a ruler.[19] Tragically, the lesson does not sink home in Act III when reconciliation appears possible, and Ottokar repeats his mistake, only to show signs of genuine moral improvement shortly before his death. Then he regrets his crimes, accusing himself of having had no respect for the human beings whom he has ill-treated and sacrificed for his own cause. These comments amount to Grillparzer's own condemnation of Ottokar's egocentric and tyrannical behavior. The Ottokar who rides roughshod over the interests of others in order to fulfill his own ambitions is another Jason, the private adventurer transferred onto the political stage. Ottokar's reassessment of his career is also strongly suggestive of the Baroque influence on Grillparzer's plays, for at this stage of the tragedy we see the penitent sinner coming to recognize the evil of his ways before submitting himself to the judgment of God.

The touchstone by which Ottokar's behavior may be judged is provided by Rudolf, who describes how as emperor he has lost all interest in himself, and is now unselfishly devoted to the interests of his peoples. The contrast between Ottokar and Rudolf is frequently stressed. In Act I Ottokar is characterized by the set and by his dress. He sits surrounded by the magnificence of his court, dressed in full armor. By contrast Rudolf is shown in a more modest light, in sympathetic conversation with Queen Margarethe. Later as emperor he is seated in his tent, dressed in simple clothes, repairing his helmet with a hammer. He cares nothing for his station or for external magnificence. Ottokar would like to think he has the more command-ing and magical personality, but it is Rudolf who is paradoxically the more magnetic figure, and it is a significant feature of the play that characters tend to desert or betray Ottokar, and gravitate toward the more humane and sympathetic Rudolf. It is Ottokar's tragedy that he acquires too late the humility and piety necessary to make him worthy of high office.

But there is more to this tragedy than this conspicuous moral theme. During their confrontation in Act III Rudolf gives a psychological explanation for Ottokar's behavior. He is convinced that in his case power itself has been a corrupting influence, exposing him to temptations and stimulating his desire for more. Rudolf's words bear a striking similarity to Grillparzer's own appraisal of the historical Otakar and of Napoleon, both of whom he felt had been driven more by circumstance than an evil nature to commit acts of tyranny (IV, 117). Margarethe and Seyfried Merenberg, a young Styrian noble at Ottokar's court, are also convinced that Ottokar is not an essentially evil man. For Margarethe he has been misled by others, notably the Rosenbergs, his "bad angels," who have cun-ningly exploited his desire for an heir, and deliberately flaunted before him their niece Bertha. According to Seyfried, Ottokar has, prior to the divorce, been a model of rectitude. During the play itself, however, we do not see this noble character. Right from the begin-ning his behavior suggests that of a man drunk with power. He is aggressive, boorish, and arrogant. He treats the friendly Tartars with contempt, brandishing their curved sword and criticizing its design to their faces. When his servants are unable to remove his shin-guard he first asks the Mayor of Prague to perform this menial task, and then rips it off himself and hurls it angrily to the ground. Exultantly he describes the extent of his lands:

> Vom Belt bis fern zum adriatschen Golf,
> Vom Inn bis zu der Weichsel kaltem Strand
> Ist niemand, der nicht Ottokarn gehorcht;
> Es hat die Welt seit Karol Magnus Zeiten
> Kein Reich noch wie das meinige gesehn.   (605–9)

(From the Baltic to the distant Adriatic, from the Inn to the cold banks of the Vistula, there is no one who does not obey Ottokar. Since the days of Charlemagne the world has seen no empire like mine.)

In Act II his behavior becomes tyrannical, and we witness the possi-ble onset of a reign of terror. Faced with treachery and defection, he can trust no one and plans to make arbitrary arrests. At times it appears that Grillparzer attempts to minimize Ottokar's guilt as far as possible. For example, when he evacuates citizens of Prague from their own homes to make way for skilled German craftsmen, he does so in order to improve the cultural and material circumstances of his peoples. But the impatience that he shows in the face of their objections, his ruthless determination to enforce a policy that he considers best, irrespective of the feelings of those involved, are typical of the despot who, however enlightened his intentions, behaves in a manner that is inhumane and positively Hitlerian. It is a foretaste of the Ottokar whom we are to see in Act III, when he contemplates the wholesale destruction of areas in which the local population has transferred its loyalty to Rudolf, and when he threatens to reduce Austria to a wasteland. During his moments of remorse before his death he castigates himself precisely on this score, for treating people like garbage with a cynical disregard for their intrinsic value as human beings. The first half of the play is ostensibly a psychological study in tyranny, in which it is Grillparzer's main concern to represent the dangerous extremes to which a man might be pushed by the corrupting influence of power. His fascination with immoral and violent behavior, already seen in Sappho and Medea, is here continued in the political forum.

But Grillparzer's portrait of the tyrant amounts to more than just a succession of wicked deeds. Occasionally, even in the early stages of the play, we glimpse a second Ottokar underneath the mask of confidence which he projects to the outer world, an Ottokar who is weaker, more human, and more vulnerable than even he himself realizes. As the first act progresses, we see that Ottokar's power has been gained more through good fortune—inheritance, marriage, and assistance, ironically from Rudolf in the recent battle—than by his own efforts. A series of dramatic incidents conveys to us the increase in his power, but this is accompanied by a simultaneous series of signals to the audience that tends to undermine his position. As the Austrian and Styrian nobles arrive in succession to offer him their ducal coronets, they first do homage to Margarethe, whom Ottokar is in the process of dismissing, so that their defection is already foreseen by us, if not by Ottokar himself. Then, as the Carinthians bring him yet another crown and Ottokar is hailed prematurely as emperor, old Merenberg, Seyfried's father, is seen sending a message to the electors which will prevent his election. The timing of this incident underlines the fact that the divorce represents a serious piece of political miscalculation.[20] Next, in one of Grillparzer's most cele-

brated dramatic episodes, we are given vivid evidence of future
developments when the emissaries from Frankfurt ask if Ottokar
would be prepared to accept the imperial crown should it be offered.
Intending to give a broad hint of the electors' intentions, the first
emissary raises aloft what he takes to be Ottokar's own shield, but
chooses not the white lion of Bohemia, but mistakenly, and propheti-
cally, the red lion of Hapsburg. At this, Ottokar is only momentarily
shaken, and he proceeds blindly on his way, still assuming that the
crown is his for the taking. This is typical of the attitude that he has
displayed throughout, for he has already reacted scornfully to Margarethe's warnings that he is surrounded by traitors, confident that he
can sweep aside anything that stands in his way. Ottokar is suffering
from delusions of grandeur, and he behaves as though his political
greatness were but a reflection of his qualities as a man.

But in the eyes of the audience the image of the all-powerful king is
somewhat tarnished, and in the second act Ottokar experiences his
first reversal with the news of Rudolf's election. Here the mask of
confidence does slip to a remarkable degree. Previous to this, Ottokar
had adopted a condescending attitude toward the electors and had
even expressed a reluctance to accept the crown. Yet when the news
comes, his behavior conveys the full extent of his disappointment.
The subtlety of Grillparzer's technique in his revelation of emotions
and states of mind is well illustrated here. Instead of having the news
conveyed to Ottokar by the formal announcement, he first has the
chancellor give the information informally to others. Ottokar is, at the
time, boldly announcing his plans for the moment when he becomes
emperor, but as he hears the chancellor's words he is visibly shocked.
His hand shakes, he stutters, he trembles at the knees, staring for a
minute into space. Rapidly he pulls himself together, attempts to
continue as though nothing had happened, and greets the public
announcement truculently. But for a moment we have been afforded
a surprising glimpse of a less confident Ottokar, a man broken by
disappointment, who has briefly come face to face with reality. It is an
Ottokar whom we shall see again later in the play. But for the time
being he resumes his confident front, his delusions return, to the
extent that he truly believes he can defy Rudolf on the field of battle.
During Act III he is reluctant to admit that Rudolf holds the upper
hand, and when he does finally agree to meet him, he assumes he will
humiliate him by the sheer force of his personality. Ironically, it is
Ottokar who is demoralized by the encounter. The first three acts
represent a process whereby Ottokar is reduced in stature, first in the

eyes. of the audience, and then in his own, when he eventually acknowledges his subservience to the man whom he has hitherto regarded as his inferior.

At this point there occurs a crucial incident which makes it psychologically impossible for Ottokar to accept this situation for long. Rudolf demands that Ottokar should kneel to him to accept the fiefs of Bohemia and Moravia, something which Ottokar is prepared to do, though within the privacy of Rudolf's tent. But when Zawisch von Rosenberg cuts down the entrance to the tent, Ottokar's humiliation becomes a public one. Public shame is something that he cannot bear, and he stands head bowed before rushing from the scene in a great rage. In Act IV we see him broken by the experience. He returns to his native Bohemia in most uncharacteristic fashion, wandering incognito and alone about the countryside. Then, instead of entering Prague with a flourish, he sits dejectedly on the steps outside the city gates, unrecognized by the mayor whom he has insulted in Act I, mocked and humiliated by his second wife Kunigunde. This image of a weaker, downcast Ottokar presents a striking contrast to the earlier one. Here is Ottokar the man, much less impressive, stripped of all pomp and glory. But Ottokar cannot reconcile the manner in which he is now treated with the old Ottokar he once was, and it is his old image that he attempts to resurrect. Unable to bear the memory of his public shame any longer—he shows an almost pathological obsession with his recollection of that moment when he was seen to kneel to Rudolf—he decides to obliterate the memory with a conscious and deliberate reassertion of his old self.[21] Again he is all defiance and bravado, refuses to comply with Rudolf's orders, dismisses Kunigunde, sends old Merenberg to the tower, and prepares for yet another military adventure. That his performance is inappropriate, both to the circumstances and the man, is subtly suggested when Ottokar proceeds to fall asleep in his chancellor's lap. Our final image of him in this act is that of the weaker mortal, cradled by the older man like a little child.

That Ottokar can never recapture his former glory is confirmed in Act V. On the military front he wavers indecisively, and there is a telling moment before the decisive battle when Ottokar thinks he has Rudolf caught like a mouse in a trap. He laughs, an indication that his delusions have returned, but his laughter is hoarse, and turns into a cough. The physical image mocks his confident words as he is caught off-guard again at a very human moment. Finally he is seen dead, naked as a beggar, his head resting once more in his chancellor's lap,

an image which provides another of Grillparzer's eloquent tes-
timonies to the futility of the pursuit of greatness and fame. It also
completes Grillparzer's exposure of this self-styled Charlemagne as a
king who, underneath his display of self-aggrandizement, is but an
ordinary mortal.

Two aspects of the tragedy that contribute to this view of Ottokar
are his relationships with his two wives, and the presentation of
Zawisch von Rosenberg. In themselves the two marriages provide
interesting and contrasting studies of relationships in which the two
parties seem particularly ill-matched. Margarethe is considerably
older than Ottokar, and has been more mother to him than wife—
there has certainly been no sexual relationship between them. But it
is in Act V when, in a highly contrived piece of theater, Ottokar
discovers her dead body near the battlefield, that we gain an inkling
of the kind of influence she exercised upon him. In a moving scene he
appeals to her for her blessing and for comfort, and even begins to
acknowledge his errors, as his spiritual communion with her fills him
with remorse and softens him. Margarethe was his moral guide, and it
was his tragic mistake that he should have repudiated her for the
younger woman. His second marriage presents a very different situation. Here the younger Kunigunde is married to the older Ottokar,
whom she soon despises as an old man. She succumbs to Zawisch's
advances, and then taunts Ottokar mercilessly when his fortunes are
low. It is quite understandable that he should respond to these taunts
by defying Rudolf once again, and the second fatal rebellion is arguably as much that of the maddened husband as of the humiliated
king.[22] Kunigunde's influence is as disastrous as Margarethe's was
beneficial, and in the final analysis Ottokar's downfall is brought
about as much by events in his domestic life as by affairs of state. The
principal function of the presentation of the two marriages is to make
Ottokar that much more pathetic a character. Mothered by Margarethe, humiliated by Kunigunde, he is in each case the weaker
partner.

The role of Zawisch in relation to Ottokar is similar. Until Act IV, to
Ottokar's face at least, he appears to offer loyal support, flattering
Ottokar's vanity, even insisting that victory over Rudolf is assured.
From the beginning he also appears to be out of sympathy with his
relatives' ambitions, mocking them over their failure to marry poor
Bertha to Ottokar. Yet, beneath the facade, he is playing a double
game. His behavior is at times enigmatic and puzzling, and his
motives are never clearly stated, but it soon becomes apparent that

his own aspirations are even more presumptuous than those of the other Rosenbergs, his intention being to undermine, and possibly even usurp, Ottokar's position as king. Early in Act II the Rosenbergs capture Seyfried Merenberg with the letter to the Archbishop of Mainz, but Zawisch allows him to escape, presumably because he too wishes to undermine Ottokar's imperial ambitions. He later encourages Ottokar in his defiance of Rudolf to the most foolhardy degree, in order to ensure Ottokar's defeat. Then it is he who cuts down the tent opening, to reveal Ottokar's shame to the world, so destroying all hope of a permanent reconciliation between Ottokar and the emperor. Zawisch is indeed Ottokar's bad angel, playing a Mephistophelian role, driving him to absurd lengths through false praise and encouragement, and thereby engineering his eventual downfall.

Zawisch is one of Grillparzer's most sinister characters, the only true villain in his plays, but an attractive, almost playful villain. Nowhere is his behavior more cynical than in his audacious wooing of Kunigunde, whom he snatches almost from under Ottokar's nose. His protestations of love are delivered in such an exaggerated, ironic, and almost jocular fashion that it is impossible to take them seriously. Much more likely is it that she simply figures in his political plans, which seem well on the way to fruition when we see him blatantly take Ottokar's place beside her in Act IV. Zawisch's success in bringing Ottokar down clearly reflects adversely on Ottokar himself, who seems vulnerable and naive in the face of the machinations of his clever adversary. He is belittled by Zawisch, who exploits and esposes his weaknesses. Ultimately, however, Zawisch is no more successful in achieving his designs than is Ottokar himself. Even before Ottokar's revival, Zawisch flees his presence, eventually to seek sanctuary with Rudolf, who gives him very short shrift indeed. Zawisch fades from the play as a further illustration of the futility of ambition, his career providing a parallel with Ottokar's own. But it is a distorted parallel, and is presented with greater irony. Zawisch pursues his aims through trickery and sexual adventure, with blatant cynicism. Through him Grillparzer makes a mockery of ambition, employing the methods of the satirist to illustrate his moral theme, and introduces the ironical, burlesque atmosphere of the Viennese popular theater.

An atmosphere of a different kind, but which is equally removed from that of the German Classical drama, is created by two brief dramatic sequences in which Grillparzer captures the effect on Bertha von Rosenberg of Ottokar's rejection of her. First, in Act IV, we see her in a deranged state, aimlessly throwing handfuls of soil about her like a child. Then, at the close of the tragedy, she reappears on the field of battle before the dead Ottokar, to knock dementedly on Margarethe's coffin with the words: "Open up, Margarethe, look, your husband is here!" It is at such moments that Grillparzer approaches the episodic style and grotesque realism achieved in the following decade by Georg Büchner, to be developed later by the dramatists of Expressionism.

In several ways *König Ottokar* represents the culmination of the early phase of Grillparzer's development. It provides a more penetrating study of the ambitious self-seeker than either *Die Ahnfrau* or *Das goldene Vlieβ*, and in treating the theme of ambition in a political, as opposed to a private, context, Grillparzer relates the theme to the specific situation of the authoritarian ruler. By representing in the character of Rudolf a standard of behavior by which the attitude and conduct of the hero may be judged, he achieves a fuller and more balanced treatment of the subject. Moreover, Rudolf's triumph enables him to end the tragedy on what is for Grillparzer a uniquely optimistic note. Yet the optimism of the final lines contrasts markedly with the atmosphere surrounding the downfall and death of Ottokar. The exposure of Ottokar's weaknesses and the reduction of this mighty king to the level of unheroic mediocrity provides an even more striking piece of theater than the similar deflation of Jason. In Ottokar, too, we have a further example of a character presented in the grip of an uncontrollable passion, which, though very different from the jealousy and hatred that inspired Sappho and Medea, is even more frightening and far-reaching in its effects. Yet, while noting the overtly moralizing elements of the tragedy, we again discern the approach of the psychologist, bent on affording his audience an insight into the character of his tyrant, providing further illustration of Grillparzer's tendency toward a more realistic dramatic form.

CHAPTER 3

The Middle Years (1826–37)

I Ein treuer Diener seines Herrn

WITH the exception of *Der Traum ein Leben* the plays of Grillparzer's middle years tend to be more problematical than the majority of his early tragedies, the new phase being introduced by *Ein treuer Diener seines Herrn* [A Faithful Servant of his Master]. Grillparzer's interest in this material dates from 1815, but had been rekindled when he was invited to write a play in celebration of the coronation of the empress as Queen of Hungary. In his pursuit of a suitable subject he researched the life of the queen of King Andreas II, Gertrudis of Meran, but it was not long before he rejected both the subject and the invitation. His interest in the period continued, however, and spread from Gertrudis to her brother Otto, and eventually to the almost mythical figure of Andreas's deputy, the Ban Bánk. In spite of its initial success, *Ein treuer Diener* has never been one of Grillparzer's more popular plays, and it is not surprising that the feature that at first satisfied the censor and apparently earned the approval of Emperor Francis should have subsequently met with the strongest criticism. This is the presentation of the hero. Bancbanus is one of Grillparzer's more "difficult" characters, and unlike anything he had created previously. He is neither a political adventurer nor a man of selfish passion, but a well-intentioned and loyal servant of his king. Consequently, Grillparzer has been accused—unjustifiably—of glorifying a mere servile man who appears to champion a fundamentally conservative loyalty to the monarchic principle.[1]

Structurally, the tragedy provides further evidence of the Baroque influence on Grillparzer in that the hero is given a mission and eventually judged by his success in fulfilling it. Bancbanus's mission is to guarantee the safety of the queen and son of King Andreas and to maintain peace and order in the kingdom during the king's temporary absence. Yet even before the king's departure there are signs that Bancbanus's task will not be easy. Ironically, it is the tranquillity of

Bancbanus's private life that is threatened, and by one of the king's own relatives, Duke Otto, the brother of Queen Gertrude, who is intent on pursuing the affections of Bancbanus's young wife Erny. Then, when Bancbanus is appointed co-regent with Gertrude, the latter is enraged that he should have been preferred to Otto. Andreas is shocked at this indication of discord, and the first act closes in an atmosphere of disquiet.

The three central acts confirm this impression in an exciting sequence of dramatic action. While Bancbanus attempts to administer affairs of state, Otto intensifies his pursuit of Erny during a dance in the royal castle, but governed by his determination to keep the peace, Bancbanus refuses to intervene. In any case, Erny rejects Otto's advances, but he eventually becomes so enraged that he orders his soldiers to take her off to his castle. In the face of this threat of violence Erny commits suicide. In the later stages of the play Bancbanus's loyalty to his mission faces its severest test. His own relatives, the counts Simon and Peter, demand bloody vengeance on Otto, but Bancbanus doggedly insists that judgment should be left for the king to pronounce on his return. When, therefore, the counts inspire a popular rebellion and storm the castle, Bancbanus actually has to protect Otto along with the queen and her little son. But though Otto and the prince escape, there is further bloodshed when the queen's dark shape is mistaken during the confusion for that of Otto, and she is killed. So when Andreas returns in Act V, Bancbanus has to face him not only with a revolutionary situation on his hands, but with the death of the queen on his conscience. Yet the king shows clemency to Simon and Peter, and to Otto, and even rewards Bancbanus for his fidelity. This not simply because he recognizes Bancbanus's good intentions, but primarily because Bancbanus has succeeded in securing the life of the little prince who will eventually succeed to the throne.

For all the king's generous praise, however, Bancbanus can be criticized on several counts, and his behavior is at times scarcely impressive. During the dance, for example, his loyalty is treated satirically, almost comically, as he attends to affairs of state in the midst of all the merry-making. He is presented with grotesque irony, as a bumbling bureaucrat, a figure of fun for courtiers and servants alike, interrupted by calls for water and lemons, and by cheeky inquiries as to whether he is the doorman of the dance. But far more serious is the fact that he is seemingly unaware that his devotion to duty is leaving his wife open to danger and embarrassment; and his relatives accuse him of being too mild and gentle (*zahm*). Bancbanus does indeed contribute somewhat naively to his own personal tragedy. After Erny's death, matters become even worse, when Bancbanus's refusal to take any action against Otto leaves him open to the charge of weakness and cowardice. He also seems powerless either to prevent or suppress his relatives' rebellion. Consequently, it is arguable that although he does indeed save the life of the little prince, he has thereby fulfilled only a part of his mission.

But this gives only a one-sided picture of Bancbanus, and overlooks the fact that Grillparzer arouses considerable sympathy for this apparently unattractive and unsuccessful hero. From the start Bancbanus displays a heroic dignity in the face of taunts and insults from Otto's followers. He adopts a policy of passive resistance, ignoring the mockery with a serene detachment or equanimity (*Gleichmut*), viewing with contempt those who ridicule him. But neither Bancbanus's serenity nor his refusal to take vengeful action against his persecutor should delude us into imagining that he does not feel keenly the wrongs that are done to him. His grief at his personal loss is intense, and the more impressive for being expressed so concisely and yet so eloquently as he kneels by Erny's body: "Oh Erny, oh my child, my dear pious child!" Bancbanus has an inner strength which enables him to transcend ridicule, to survive cruel misfortune, and to remain faithful to his principles, and which befits the true martyr.

Of the other characters in the play, Duke Otto is the one who resembles most the heroes of Grillparzer's early tragedies, and the contrast between himself and Bancbanus is expressed initially in the language of the two characters. Bancbanus's speeches are noteworthy for their modesty and terseness, their attention to practical matters, with occasional words of wisdom, caustic remarks, colloquialisms, even proverbial-sounding couplets. His language has a folksy quality, wise yet unpretentious, the language of a man certain in his principles. Otto, on the other hand, is extravagant and rhetorical, producing an excited stream of emotional assertions. In his pursuit of Erny he displays the flamboyant self-confidence of Jason and Ottokar, and his subsequent collapse at his failure is even more dramatic than theirs. Otto's vanity is such that, having perceived in Erny the slightest trace of a sexual interest, he convinces himself that she is harboring a secret passion. Yet it is not her refusal to surrender to him that destroys his composure, but her sudden outburst of contempt ("I despise you!"), and his reaction suggests that behind his vanity there lies a weaker man who is basically unsure of himself. He hurls himself to the ground in a fit of rage, tearing at the floor with his bare hands.

When we next see him he appears to have suffered a nervous collapse. He lies in a feverish state in his darkened room, refuses all food
and drink, hurls a knife at the servant who tries to bleed him, and
throws himself about the bed like a spoilt child.

His pathological preoccupation with Erny's expression of contempt
is reminiscent of Ottokar's obsession with kneeling, and when he
rallies to face Erny again, he appeals to her now for her sympathy and
regard. But when she reasserts her contempt, his rage is all the
greater, and his savage instructions to his followers represent not an
attempt at abduction, but a desire to obliterate in darkness one who
has humiliated him. By Act IV it appears that Erny's death has driven
Otto insane. He is barely conscious of what has happened, has
hallucinations, thinks he sees Erny, "the pale countess," in the
corner, and when danger threatens he clings to his sister for safety.
But Grillparzer insisted that his state was not one of madness, but a
transient period of imbecility (Blödsinn).[2] Otto has been temporarily
numbed by the tragedy, and the escape with Bancbanus through the
darkness, then the responsibility of saving the child, gradually brings
him back to consciousness. That he has been totally chastened by his
experiences is indicated when he appears before the king, to produce
only a few monosyllables and to depart with a low bow, in silence. As a
figure, Otto has been seen as another representative of the futility of
pride and ambition, or of the dangers of an all-absorbing passion, but
Grillparzer's purpose here was not simply to create yet another
morally reprehensible character, but to present the disintegration of
a personality shaken by the tragic effects of his own selfishness.

The other two characters important for the dramatic action are the
queen and Erny, and here Grillparzer has provided further evidence
of his talent for creating interesting female roles. The queen is
dominated by an abnormally fierce passion for her brother. She has
worshipped Otto since childhood as the man she could never be, and
now she does all in her power to further his political and sexual
interests. In presenting her support for one so lacking in moral fiber
(Sitte), in spite of her misgivings regarding his rashness and foolhar-
diness, her tendency, then, to allow her emotions to obscure her
better judgment, Grillparzer is suggesting the character of Andreas's
court by offering a singularly unflattering picture of two of its leading
lights. It is this aspect of the play that may have led to the eventual
displeasure of Grillparzer's own emperor.

In his portrait of the queen Grillparzer develops further his technique of delineating his characters in particularly expressive visual
episodes. She is first seen clad only in her nightclothes, beside the

king who is in full armor, and whom she begs to remain longer in her chamber. Here there is a hint of sensuality in her, of slovenliness, and of a disregard for the dignity of office, for she remains dressed like this before the assembled court. The tendency to allow such episodes to speak visually for themselves testifies to the influence of Lope de Vega, whom Grillparzer had recently begun to study, and for whom plasticity or memorable scenic detail was such a high ideal.

Finally, we must consider the characterization of Erny, "one of the most astounding revelations of woman's nature in literature,"[3] and the character in this play who comes closest to experiencing a genuine inner conflict. Certainly Otto is convinced that she is battling between her duty to her husband and a secret passion for him, though it has generally been held that her feelings for Otto are no more than latent, even subconscious.[4] To his face she indeed fervently denies that she feels anything for him other than hatred and contempt, and insists that she both honors and loves her ageing husband. Yet she has given Otto several small indications of a conscious interest, a glance betraying pleasure in his appearance, a press of the hand during a dance. She even stole a lock of his hair. During the dance in Act II Grillparzer suggests that she suffers conflicting feelings of excitement and guilt. She leaves the dance in a frenzy (*erhitzt*), and dares not return to it, then trembles in fear before writing to Otto to grant him the interview he requests, even feeling guilty at holding the as yet blank piece of paper in her hand. No wonder Bancbanus feels there is something for which he must forgive her, and she comes close to a confession of guilt when she buries her head in shame in his arms. Erny's tragedy is to have married a man three times her age at a time when she was too young to understand her true nature as a woman. This Otto has aroused, and when she begins to sense this she feels only guilt and fear at the possible consequences. It is this fear that tragically takes possession of her in Act III, leading her to misunderstand both Otto's appeal for her regard and his violent reaction to her scorn, and to take her own life.

With the events of the three central acts of the tragedy Grillparzer has returned to a prominent theme of his earlier tragedies, that of passion, but here combining it with the major political theme of *König Ottokar*. Attempts have been made to find the unifying factor in this play, and Konrad Schaum has, for example, suggested that Grillparzer's aim here was to present a situation in which the stability or order of the state finds itself threatened by the forces of instability, embodied in the passions of Otto, Gertrude, and Erny, and in the violence of the rebellion, all of which represent the elemental forces

of life.[5] Certainly human passions are again represented as destructive, yet they are not to be blamed entirely for the catastrophes which
occur, and both Bancbanus and Andreas must bear their share of the
responsibility.

Bancbanus's policy of passive resistance may be admirable in some
respects. Moreover, his advice to Erny that she should avoid Otto
rather than provoke him through open defiance, is sound in view of
later developments, but it does suggest a lack of understanding of the
personalities involved. Later events also support the argument that he
should have taken a firmer line with Otto. From the beginning the
manner in which Bancbanus approaches his task raises doubts as to
his suitability for the role. He himself confesses that he is not up to it,
and begs Andreas to change his mind. Yet Andreas pays no heed to
this, and as he admits afterwards, makes the crucial mistake of leaving
Otto unrestrained behind him. Here, then, we have a situation in
which a well-intentioned monarch makes a simple error of judgment,
and in which the personality of the man left in a position of authority is
unsuited to the role. In this there is certainly a hint that the liberally
inclined dramatist is casting a doubt over the conduct of a monarchy
in which such a situation can arise.

The most harrowing result of Bancbanus's policy is the ruin of his
own domestic happiness, and it is the tragedy's most cruel irony that
in placing unselfish devotion to peace above all personal considera-
tions, he should both sacrifice the life of his wife and protect her
tormentor. Admittedly, his decision to resist his relatives' demands
for instant vengeance is justifiable on the grounds that they have
taken the law into their own hands, and that their rebellion amounts
to a bloody and barbarous vendetta against Otto, but we are nevertheless made to feel sympathetic toward the *emotions* of the rebels
through our sense of outrage at what has occurred—so much so that
the picture of Bancbanus protecting his worst enemy from forces
sympathetic to his own cause is an incongruous one, and suggests that
he is taking the principle of unselfish devotion to duty too far. It is at
this point that the play becomes truly problematic. The situation in
which Bancbanus is placed has all the ingredients of a dilemma,
requiring a clear choice between self-interest, involving a betrayal of
his principles on the one hand, and duty, involving the denial of his
feelings on the other. Bancbanus's principles show him the way
clearly out of this situation, but it is uncertain whether his attitude
should earn him our admiration or pity. From the beginning
Bancbanus is one of Grillparzer's most ambivalent characters. He

displays a heroic devotion to duty and an admirable inner strength, yet we can only regret that these qualities should have the most tragic of consequences. Significantly, Bancbanus is not the only character for whom the course of duty involves a personal sacrifice. King Andreas, too, indicates that the monarch is required by the nature of his office to subordinate personal feelings to the needs of the state, and as a figure he resembles the impersonal symbol embodied by the Rudolf of *König Ottokar*. Like Bancbanus, Andreas, too, suffers the loss of his wife, yet feels that this is compensated by the salvation of the child who will succeed him to the throne. It is disturbing that the satisfaction felt over the preservation of this monarchy should outweigh the grief felt over the tragic loss of human life, and it is appropriate that Bancbanus should close this tragedy with words that are tinged with irony, as he bows over the hand of the young prince:

> Da tat ein alter Mann—was er vermochte.
> I nu! ein treuer Diener seines Herrn.

(An old man simply did—what he could. God forbid! A faithful servant of his master.)

In *Ein treuer Diener* the issues are far less clear-cut than in *König Ottokar*. Here Grillparzer treats the same value upheld so unambiguously in his previous tragedy, that of an unselfish devotion to the state, but presents it in a far more dubious light, and the tragedy closes in an atmosphere of unease which contrasts strikingly with the optimism of its predecessor.

II   Des Meeres und der Liebe Wellen

Grillparzer had been attracted to the Hero and Leander theme as early as 1820, but it was not until 1826 that he began to work seriously on what was to be his only real tragedy of love. The stimulus for the new venture was his passion for Marie von Smolenitz, and as he composed the play he had her constantly in mind. But though Marie, like Charlotte before her, proved a fruitful model for psychological scrutiny, she was scarcely an inspiration for spontaneous creativity. Indeed, the creative difficulties that he had experienced over this play were the worst he had known so far, and *Des Meeres und der Liebe Wellen* [The Waves of the Sea and of Love] was not completed until 1829. Even then he was not really satisfied, and the failure of the premiere when it was eventually performed in 1831 did not totally surprise him. Its failure was, however, partly due to the performance of the lead actress, and it was revived successfully in 1851, thereafter to become, along with *König Ottokar* and *Der Traum ein Leben,* one of his most frequently performed plays. But dramatically it produces an effect very different from either the spectacular historical tragedy or the play written in the more popular style. *Des Meeres und der Liebe Wellen* is a sensitive adaptation of Greek legend, reminiscent both atmospherically and formally of *Sappho,* noteworthy primarily for its enchanting poetry, its delicate use of imagery, and its visual dramatic sequences, which testify once more to the growing influence of Lope de Vega on Grillparzer's dramatic style. Indeed, it so charms the senses and engages the emotions that it has rightly claimed its place as Grillparzer's most "poetic" and moving tragedy.

Structurally, this tragedy possesses the same kind of simplicity as *Sappho.* The center of the stage is occupied by another of Grillparzer's masterly female portraits, and each act of the play corresponds to a clearly defined phase in her development. Act I presents the psychological background to Hero's decision to enter the celibate life of priestess. As she prepares for her ceremony of induction, Grillparzer suggests in one of his most impressive pieces of sustained irony that her decision is dangerously unwise. Of prime importance is the fact that she has an inadequate conception of what the priesthood entails. She lacks the spiritual enthusiasm of her uncle the priest, regarding the office only as a simple and pleasant round of practical tasks, and approaches the ceremony itself as an excited young bride looks forward to her wedding day, hoping that the weather will be suitably fine to show her off at her best. She is also blissfully unaware that she is depriving herself irrevocably of the pleasures of earthly love and domestic happiness. It is not simply that she is so immature that her potentialities for love have not yet been aroused, but her experiences of life have taught her to suppress her natural inclinations. Her brother's young friends have repelled rather than attracted her, and she sees that her timid mother gets little joy from her marriage to Hero's boorish and domineering father. Consequently, the sheltered life of the temple seems to Hero like a haven from life's troubles. Just how naively limited is her view is confirmed at the close of the first act, when Grillparzer engineers the tragic coincidence of Hero's first sight of Leander with the ceremony of induction. In a supremely ironic scene Hero begins to fall in love at the very moment when she "officially" bids farewell to love and marriage, and the eventual collapse of her resolution is signalled even as she takes her vows. In itself the scene provides a striking example of psychological realism, in that the dramatically sudden effect that the figure of Leander has on Hero is conveyed not through any conscious declaration of interest on her part, but indirectly, through her confused behavior. As she sees Leander, she hesitates, bungles her words, and so loses control that she pours too much incense on the fire, which blazes up, providing an obvious symbol of the passion that has been ignited inside her. But more directly expressive of her feelings is the look that she gives Leander as she leaves, which for Naukleros, Leander's friend, amounts to a blatant confession of erotic desire. Then, as she leaves, her curiosity is such that she turns for a second look, pretending that something is wrong with her shoe. From this incident the "true" Hero has been created, a simple girl of flesh and blood under the influence of the most natural of emotions, and it is tragically inappropriate that she is soon to be judged by the harsh laws of the temple world.

During the second and third acts Hero encounters Leander again, first after the ceremony in the temple grove, and then that night when he swims the Hellespont and climbs into her room in the tower. In these two scenes Grillparzer depicts the growth of her feelings from her initial erotic interest into love, beginning with a gentle, maternal concern for his safety, compassion for him when she learns of his feelings toward her, nostalgic thoughts of him when she believes him to be far away, then anger that he should come and disturb her peace again. These are the ingredients of a love that develops gradually until Hero's sudden moment of insight as she realizes that her overriding feeling is of terror at the dangers he risks to reach her. The process of falling in love is handled more subtly than in *Das goldene Vließ,* more movingly too, as when the full tragedy of the situation is conveyed in its stark simplicity:

> Ich bin verlobt zu einem strengen Dienst,
> Und liebeleer heischt man die Priesterin.
> Ehgestern, wenn du kamst, war ich noch frei,
> Nun ists zu spät.   (1127–30)

(I am wedded to a rigorous office, demanding of the priestess a loveless life. Only yesterday, when you came, I was still free, now it is too late.)

All this time Hero has indeed attempted to fight her emotions because of the demands of her office, but finally her resistance is broken, all inner conflict is past, and at the climax of the tragedy she surrenders utterly with her famous appeal to Leander to visit her again: "Then come tomorrow!"

After her night of physical love the Hero of Act IV is a changed person. It was Grillparzer's intention to depict her now as a mature woman, whose sensuality has been aroused and who possesses a new self-assurance, oblivious to outside pressures (SB I, 19, 231–2). Certainly her preoccupation with Leander gives rise to a marked decrease in her interest in her priestly duties, and the priest himself has to intervene, believing wrongly that he can still save her from the ultimate indiscretion and preserve her for the priesthood. As Hero sleeps the next night and Leander swims to her again, the guiding light in her tower is extinguished and Leander perishes in the stormy seas. As his body is discovered on the shore and is borne away, Hero too dies. Her death is not the sudden dramatic suicide of a Sappho, but the culmination of a gradual and seemingly natural process. This is Grillparzer's most strikingly original contribution to the myth, as the traditional death of a broken heart is brought about through Hero's own complete identification with her lover:

> Sein Atem war die Luft, sein Aug die Sonne,
> Sein Leib die Kraft der sprossenden Natur,
> Sein Leben war das Leben, deines, meins,
> Des Weltalls Leben. Als wirs ließen sterben
> Da starben wir mit ihm.   (1976–80)

(His breath was the air, his eye the sun, his body the strength of burgeoning nature, his life was life itself, your life, mine, the life of the universe. When we let it die, we died, too.)

Hero's death is symbolic of the power of love which has led first to the collapse of her resolve and ultimately to her loss of life. Consequently, it is tempting to assume that love is here presented as a dangerous force, causing Leander to behave recklessly and Hero to betray her mission.[6] But, briefly, the power of love has brought Hero to full maturity and has enriched her life, giving her a second being to care for and possess:

> Und kehrst du heim, Leander,
> Das Meer durchschwimmend, nächtig, wie du kamst;
> So wahre dieses Haupt, und diesen Mund,
> Und diese meine Augen.   (1230–3)

(And when you go home, Leander, swimming through the sea by night, as you came, then take care of this head and these lips, and of these, my own eyes.)

It has also transformed the passive and insipid Leander into an immortal hero. Love is a power both dangerous and splendid, and nowhere previously in Grillparzer's works have human passions, the life forces, been presented with such sympathy and enthusiasm.

The question remains as to whether Hero can be blamed morally for her betrayal of her vows. In the eyes of the priest at least she is in danger of committing an unpardonable breach of the rules, and some commentators have also regarded the collapse of her resolution in the light of a fall from grace.[7] Such a moralistic view is encouraged by the attitude taken by the priest to his calling, and particularly by his conception of the ideal of *Sammlung,* a visionary state affording an intimate communion with the gods, to which members of the priest-hood should aspire, and which may be achieved through nocturnal spiritual contemplation and a repression of all desires of the flesh. Because of Grillparzer's own reverence for *Sammlung* as a state of concentration necessary for his work as an artist, it has been assumed that it is here presented as an absolute value, as a state of being affording fulfillment of man's most sublime aspirations. Such a high appraisal of *Sammlung* would suggest that Hero, in being sidetracked by Leander, has lost her way and missed her higher goal. It would suggest further that the irresistible passions that Grillparzer apparently so distrusted, and that he depicted so critically in earlier plays, have here claimed a further victim. In this respect it is particularly tempting to make comparisons with *Sappho,* for Sappho's own surrender to her natural emotions involves a betrayal of her calling, itself a loftier and apparently ideal mode of existence. The realms of art and of the temple seem to be closely associated in their elevation above the domain of ordinary life, the common rut, as the priest puts it so disparagingly to Hero's mother. But such comparisons are misleading, for whereas Sappho is a genuine artist, and does indeed offend against the strictures of her true calling, Hero is scarcely a "true" priestess. Her own inadequate conception of her office falls far short of the priest's ideal, and she aspires not at all to the spiritual ecstasies of *Sammlung.* Hero's unsuitability for the priesthood is also apparent from the swiftness and totality of her surrender to love. Far from missing her way, she finds it, tragically, too late. For these reasons it would seem unjust to condemn her for her surrender to her emotions. The real error is made when she takes her vows, and even here she may be excused, for her viewpoint at this time is so naively limited.

But if Hero differs from Sappho in her lack of aptitude for her calling, there are nevertheless clear parallels between the situations in which the two women find themselves. Though a genuine poetess, Sappho has felt that her calling involves an intolerable sacrifice in the form of a suppression of her natural inclinations. Hero the priestess would be similarly deprived, and the ideal of *Sammlung* turns out to be not an absolute value, but an artificial, sterile ideal, conceived only by the priest for the most select and exceptional beings, and in this case it would prevent, rather than assist, the fulfillment of Hero's true self. This does not necessarily mean that the priest's own *actions* are being condemned in the same strong terms as those used by Ianthe, the servant girl, at the close of the tragedy, or earlier by Naukleros, who accuses the priest of selfishness, arbitrary severity, and undue harshness. Even though he does bear a direct responsibility for Leander's death, the priest is only acting in accordance with his conscience as the representative of what *he* regards as an ideal mode of existence. It is the limitations of the ideal that Grillparzer is exposing in this play, not those of its individual representative. For these reasons the work can be regarded as another of Grillparzer's more problematic plays. In *Ein treuer Diener* he had cast doubt on the value of the principle of unselfish devotion to the state. Now he exposes the shortcomings of the apparently ideal order of the priesthood, and opposes to it the natural and intrinsically beautiful value of human love. And just as an exclusive devotion to her art had its disadvantages for Sappho's natural self, so do the laws of celibacy imposed by the priesthood involve the denial of vital aspects of human nature. At the same time the indulgence of these dangerously irresistible natural forces prove in both *Sappho* and *Des Meeres und der Liebe Wellen* to have disastrous consequences. In his treatment of the major themes we may discern again traces of Grillparzer's own perplexing situation. A man capable of experiencing to the full the most enriching of emotions, he nevertheless recognized the dangers of human passions; believing also that he must devote himself to what he conceived as his own higher calling, he knew that an over-exclusive dedication could involve an intolerable personal sacrifice. Although the thematic content of the tragedy may reflect some of Grillparzer's darker problems, some of its most memorable scenes have a far different effect. The festive atmosphere of the opening scene, for example, makes a strikingly bright impression, with its sunshine, blue sky, wide open spaces, white statues and floral decorations, matched by Hero's own sunny and confident mood. The immediate impression suggests the dramatist's sense of the beauty of life and youth. A similarly expressive scene occurs in Act I when a dove is discovered in its nest in the temple grounds. A slave is made to remove both bird and nest, for such manifestations of natural animal behavior are here taboo, but Hero takes the nest from the slave and caresses the dove, finally handing it over to be taken to its freedom. This whole sequence is charged with symbolic import, anticipating in various ways the future course of the tragedy, but the scene's main expressive power comes from Hero's own gentleness and maternal compassion for the dove, which clearly indicate that she is more in harmony with the natural life of the dove than with the exalted and aloof existence of priestess, and suggest her potentiality for love. The sympathy with which Grillparzer treats her manner, which is contrasted with the uncompromisingly strict attitude of the priest, is here indicative of his warm appreciation for the natural processes of life. The dove scene also provides a good example of Grillparzer's sensitive attention to the visual side of drama, of the plasticity of his style. Another example occurs on the evening following the ceremony when Hero removes the priestly robe. As she does so, she remarks that she is thereby shedding all that she would wish to forget from the events of this day. From her previous words it is evident that what she wishes to put behind her are the feelings Leander aroused in her. What the audience sees, however, is the figure of a young girl, casting off the priestess robe and the unnatural restrictions which it implies, soon to follow her natural inclinations in a night of physical love. The truth of the situation is here expressed by visual symbol, and not by Hero's ironically inappropriate words. Here also Grillparzer is showing his appreciation of the physical charms of youth and beauty, and he does so again through Naukleros's description of Leander's body, an apparently perfect example of the male form:

> Ein Junge, schön, wenngleich nicht groß, und braun.
> Die finstern Locken ringeln um die Stirn;
> Das Auge, wenns die Wimper nicht verwehrt,
> Sprüht heiß wie Kohle, frisch nur angefacht;
> Die Schultern weit; die Arme derb und tüchtig,
> Von prallen Muskeln ründlich überragt. (580–5)

(A handsome youth, though not tall, and dark-skinned. His brow surrounded
by dark curls. Through his eyelashes his eyes sparkle like hot coals, newly
fanned into flame; his shoulders broad, his arms strong and sturdy, each
crowned by firm, round muscles.)

Here is the Greek Classical ideal of physical beauty, opposed so
positively in this play to the spiritual ideal of the priest.

Grillparzer's attention to visual and physical detail is also matched
by the imagery of the play. Much has already been written on this
aspect of the work, in which "the abstract is repeatedly lent concrete
form by the close interlocking of the symbols and images with the
stage picture."[8] Particularly striking is his use of light imagery, which
takes on visible concrete form in the lamp that Hero lights to guide
Leander to her like a star in the night, and that is so treated as to
represent visually the flickering of her passion. The power of love is
also associated metaphorically with the waves of the sea. This association is suggested first by the evocative title of this tragedy, and
continued—particularly in frequent references during the love scene
in Act III—to the wild sea whose every ripple may bring death, to the
violently seething sea, the sea whose gentle waves may at one moment offer a pleasant bath, but at another may make the onlooker
dizzy with the evidence of their destructive power. The fickle character of the sea conveyed in these images becomes a poetic extension of
the capricious nature of love, which can be so enriching and intrinsically valuable and yet so destructive. Love, as the title suggests, may
be likened to a wave, sweeping over the individual and metaphorically drowning him. It is the tragedy of Hero and Leander that they
fall under its sway in the most unpropitious circumstances, thereby
coming into conflict with an institution whose ideals are so uncompromising in their demands.

III   Der Traum ein Leben

After his long preoccupation with Greek legend and historical
tragedy it may seem surprising that Grillparzer should have next
produced a play in the style of the Viennese popular theater. But in
fact the conception of *Der Traum ein Leben* [A Dream is Life] goes
back as far as 1817, when Grillparzer had just completed the successful *Ahnfrau* and was still interested in writing in a similar mode.
Thereafter, the plan was put aside, to be resurrected when he returned from Germany in 1826; and the first version was finally completed in 1830. In his autobiography Grillparzer suggests that it was

primarily for therapeutic reasons that he persisted in this project, for its colorful and lively material was well suited to bring him out of his despondency of the late 1820s (IV, 162). Yet it is also possible that, in returning to a dramatic form that had brought him early popularity, he was once again seeking success and recognition after his run of disappointments. Certainly, after enjoying a successful premiere in 1834, *Der Traum* received more performances at the Burgtheater in Grillparzer's lifetime than any other of his plays. Its spectacular settings, the lightness of its tone, and the verve of its poetry had an immediate appeal. Though employing the same trochaic verse form as *Die Ahnfrau*, the play is entirely different in mood. In the early stages we have a sunlit evening in idyllic surroundings, while the central part of the action takes place in the fairy-tale world of action and adventure. Here there are obvious links with the world of the Viennese *Zauberstücke* ("plays of magic") with their supernatural figures. Grillparzer had already ventured into this field in 1823 when he wrote *Melusina*, a libretto for an opera requested originally by Beethoven. *Melusina* is a highly romantic fairy-tale operetta, presenting the love of a mortal for a fairy, set in woodland glades and in Melusina's ethereal realm, with songs and dancing, nymphs and spirits, and supernatural effects. But *Der Traum ein Leben* is less fanciful and the main influence upon it was the *Besserungsstück*, ("play of correction") another traditional genre of the popular stage in which the main character undergoes a process of moral improvement (*Besserung*).

The influence on *Der Traum ein Leben* of the *Besserungsstück* is discernible primarily in its framework structure. Here the frame is provided by the desires of the central character, Rustan, to break out of the narrow confines of his peaceful country existence in pursuit of glory and power. The central events of the play embody a dream which reveals to Rustan just what such a life may entail, and as a result he decides when he awakens to remain in his present state after all, having effectively learnt his lesson. In the fantastic world of the dream Rustan is raised to a position of eminence through falsely taking credit for saving the King of Samarkand from a deadly serpent. But to cover his tracks he has to kill the real rescuer, the mysterious "man on the rock," and the dream turns into a nightmare when the body is found. Rustan is cross-examined, and to protect himself again he has to murder the king. Although he recovers his position briefly and marries the princess Gulnare, he eventually has to flee the kingdom, finally plunging from a bridge, to wake up at home in his own bed. The dream represents a life of deception and murder, and

the well-worn early Grillparzer theme of the futility of ambition is
struck again in the famous lines of Rustan's conclusion:

> Eines nur ist Glück hienieden,
> Eins, des Innern stiller Frieden
> Und die schuldbefreite Brust.
> Und die Größe ist gefährlich,
> Und der Ruhm ein leeres Spiel.   (2650–4)

(In this world there is only one true happiness, just one, the quiet peace of
one's inner self and a breast free of guilt. And greatness is dangerous, and
fame a hollow game.)

Like Medea's similar conclusion at the close of *Das goldene Vließ*
these words provide a moral commentary on the aspirations of the
hero.

Rustan's desire for glory in the great outside world has been
compared with the strivings for uplifting experience of Goethe's
Faust. Rustan's aspirations, like Faust's, involve him in guilt and evil,
and the flames of his desires are fanned by the temptations of a
mocking Mephistophelian figure, offered here by his servant Zanga,
an obvious extension of the playful and apparently harmless Zawisch,
who behaved with such insidious duplicity in luring Ottokar to his
downfall. But Rustan's conclusion, an affirmation of the values of the
narrow simple life which he has previously rejected, is scarcely
Faustian and has been frequently used to identify the essential difference between the active and "positive" Goethe and the resigned,
"negative" Grillparzer. Thus Rustan's words have become identified
with Grillparzer's own philosophy, suggesting a recognition of the
dangers of man's active or vital impulses, and stressing the need for a
retreat from the affairs of the world as a means of protecting one's
innocence. Grillparzer's own disappointments may at times have led
him to adopt such a gloomy attitude, but as W. E. Yates has effectively
argued, Rustan's conclusion need not necessarily be taken as an
expression of Grillparzer's own consistent view.[9] It has, indeed,
simply been seen as an embodiment of the Biedermeier ideal of a
modest, unenterprising, and resigned, but essentially contented acceptance of one's limited station in life.

But the key to the play, as Erich Hock's stimulating essay first
showed, lies in Rustan's character.[10] Rustan is essentially a weak
man, whose aspirations are exaggerated far beyond his own capabili-
ties. He boasts enthusiastically of what he hopes to achieve, but he

needs Zanga's leadership to put his ideas into practice. It is Zanga who shows him how to turn the incident of the serpent to his own advantage, who urges him to deceive and lie, for Rustan lacks courage and becomes desperately alarmed when things begin to go wrong. Rustan is a second Ottokar rather than an Austrian Faust, a man whose ambitions outstrip his ability, and when he does attain power we see him become, like Ottokar, a tyrant, clinging to his own false position. As with Ottokar, we have an unmasking of the would-be hero, a process which Zdenko Škreb has aptly termed *Entheroisierung*.[11] The dream gives him an insight into his own true value, and Rustan is made to realize that his real place lies within the confines of his own circle in a state of rural domestic bliss. The dream is a process of self-discovery, not a representation of a universal truth, and although the somewhat hackneyed Biedermeier moral emerges, familiar to all Viennese audiences of the time, it is here applied most fittingly to a particular man.

In *Der Traum ein Leben* Grillparzer treats a popular theme without necessarily conferring universal validity on the play's concluding moral. But the theme is treated with obvious clarity, and the "message" emerges unambiguously from the central section in accordance with the tradition of the popular theater. Grillparzer did not wish to banish ideas from art altogether, but sought to communicate them in concrete terms. This he does in *Der Traum* through the medium of the dream, and Rustan's conclusion merely confirms what has already been made clear through dramatic action. Though this *Besserungsstück* is technically a "problem play," it is not really problematic, but belongs essentially to Grillparzer's earlier period, rather than to the more "difficult" plays of the middle phase of his development.

But if *Der Traum ein Leben* is thematically one of Grillparzer's lighter works, it is nonetheless a skillful piece of dramatic writing. Particularly striking is Grillparzer's handling of the dream sequence itself, which is so constructed as to suggest that it is really a projection of images already present in Rustan's mind, and inspired by his own real-life experiences. Characters in the dream are based on the characters whom we meet in the first act. The king whom Rustan deceives and kills is the dream counterpart of Rustan's uncle Massud, whose protection Rustan is threatening to renounce. The original of the princess Gulnare, whom Rustan marries under false pretences, is the simple peasant girl Mirza, whose affections he is spurning. Grillparzer has thus transformed Rustan's attitudes into behavior which, in the exaggerated world of the dream, is dramatically more noxious, so suggesting the subconscious twinges of Rustan's conscience. Similarly, the man on the rock has his counterpart in Osmin, the aristocrat who sneers at Rustan's lack of achievement, and the fight on the bridge is a projection of the real-life quarrel between Rustan and Osmin. But more than this, the real achievement of the man in killing the serpent suggests Rustan's dim awareness of his own weakness. The dream is an exercise in depth psychology, a dramatic projection of the glimmerings of truth which are latent in Rustan's subconscious mind. As well as giving the dream psychological credibility, Grillparzer also tries to create a convincing impression of a genuine nightmare. This is conveyed particularly by the changing forms of the threatening figures of the man on the rock, by the confusion of Rustan's flight amidst fire and fighting, and finally by the sheer terror of the dream's conclusion, as Rustan is trapped on all sides by his pursuers. Particularly realistic is Rustan's awakening from the dream, which begins when the chiming of the clock in Massud's cottage penetrates Rustan's sleep, and culminates in the plunge from the bridge, conveying the familiar sensation of falling at the end of a nightmare. The psychological realism with which the dream sequence is presented compensates for the absence of subtle characterization, usually such a prominent feature of Grillparzer's plays.

Ostensibly, however, the main emphasis in the dream sequence is on exciting action and spectacle, and it is this that links the play most closely with the popular stage. At times, action is poorly motivated. The dream commences with the fortuitous encounter with the King of Samarkand, and the rise in Rustan's fortunes is unbelievably swift, but Viennese audiences were accustomed to the improbable world of the *Zauberstück* and readily accepted such imperfections. Typical of the *Zauberstück*, too, is Grillparzer's use of standard motifs which contribute to the visual appeal and the plasticity (*Bildlichkeit*) of the play. Prominent are the bridge which divides the world of fantasy from that of reality, the serpent which pursues the king, the dagger with which Rustan kills the man, and the witch's cup from which the king drinks his poison. The dramatic function of the witch is to tempt Rustan to murder at a vital stage in the plot, but she also has a symbolic significance, representing the forces of evil to which Rustan is subject. Similarly, old Kaleb, the dumb father of the man on the rock, who regains his speech to denounce Rustan as the king's murderer, represents the irresistible forces of truth and goodness which eventually gain dominion over Rustan's soul. These grotesque fairy-tale figures have an allegorical function, embodying the drama that is taking place in the sleeping Rustan's soul.

The psychological significance given to the events of the dream is an attempt by Grillparzer to adapt popular theater elements to the aesthetic requirements of the Burgtheater. At the time, there was a clear division in Vienna between the leading authorities and popular taste, and the attempts of the former to introduce a more refined, cultured, dramatic style came into conflict with the popular desire for entertainment. In combining elements of the *Zauberstück* with the precepts of "literary" drama, Grillparzer successfully bridges the gap between the popular and serious theater of his day. Nowhere is this more apparent than in the language of this play, which though occasionally colloquial in tone (*vide* the frequent omission of unstressed syllables and endings, and the use of short exclamations such as "ei!," "wohl!," and "ob auch!"), has at times a poetic beauty envied particularly by Ferdinand Raimund. The opening scene, for example, constitutes a sensitive, if somewhat conventional, attempt to capture the peace and solemnity of a summer evening. Grillparzer was himself only too conscious of the unique qualities of his play, for which there is no comparable model in the Classical repertoire. But he felt that the experiment did not bear repetition, and so enjoyed his last success on the Viennese stage (see G I, 5).

IV Weh dem, der lügt!

Encouraged by the success of *Der Traum ein Leben*, Grillparzer turned again to a more popular genre, comedy, a mode which one might justifiably suppose to have been foreign to his nature. But among the substantial body of unpublished material found after his death are numerous satirical sketches testifying to his ability to step outside his personal problems and the imperfections of his environment, and to view them with a somewhat sardonic humor. Furthermore, the satirical elements in the presentation of such characters as Bancbanus, or the father of Hero in *Des Meeres und der Liebe Wellen*, do suggest a talent for comedy, which at length bore fruit in *Weh dem, der lügt!* [Woe unto him who Lies]. This comedy has the same framework structure associated with the popular theater as *Der Traum ein Leben*, in that the hero sets off on a journey at the beginning of the play, and returns at the conclusion. But here the central events are not designed to teach the hero a lesson, but represent the attempts of the hero to fulfill a particular task. Here,

then, is the same formula as that used in *Ein treuer Diener*. But the
hero of *Weh dem, der lügt!*, the simple kitchen-boy Leon, is singularly more successful in his activities that either Bancbanus or Rustan, and fortune smiles on his enterprise from the beginning. Leon's
task is to rescue for his master, Bishop Gregory of Chalons, the latter's
nephew Atalus, who is held hostage by barbarian enemies across the
Rhine. However, Leon's mission is made even more difficult by the
crucial condition set by the bishop, namely, that he must speak the
truth at all times, for the bishop's ethic condemns the lie as the worst
form of evil. Leon achieves his objective and returns unscathed with
Atalus, having adhered to the bishop's condition to the letter. But,
though he does not lie, he nevertheless resorts to various ruses and
pieces of trickery, and deceives Atalus's captors through his behavior,
if not through his words.

Atalus is held by Count Kattwald, into whose household Leon first
worms his way by pretending to be a slave and ingeniously having
himself sold to Kattwald as a cook, at a suitably high price. Once
installed, he makes contact with Atalus and organizes their escape. A
feast in Kattwald's hall, for which he spices the food to encourage
maximum consumption of wine, enables him to take advantage of his
master's drunkenness to attempt to steal the key to the outer gate.
Eventually, with help from Kattwald's own daughter Edrita, he and
Atalus slip away. Leon is an enterprising opportunist who uses his
wits and ingenuity, but hardly in the *spirit* of the bishop's condition.
Truthfulness alone would have been of no avail, so Leon has to resort
to some form of subterfuge to achieve success. For that reason, and
because Leon's behavior is presented so attractively, his expediency
appears to contrast favorably with the bishop's uncompromising
abstract idealism. Gregor is cast in the same mold as the priest in *Des
Meeres und der Liebe Wellen*, and is another of Grillparzer's highly
principled advocates of an absolute value, which is once again opposed to more human values. In Act I the bishop even shows that he
would rather sacrifice Atalus than betray his principles, and his stern
moralizing comes across as sterile and inhumane. But in the world of
comedy the attitude is not sustained to the bitter end, for when Leon
returns with Atalus, Gregor displays a new tolerance in his assumption that Leon has indeed lied his way out:

> Ha, du mein toller Bursch. Mein Wackrer, Treuer!
> Hier meine Hand! Nicht küssen, drücken—So.
> Nu, hübsch gelogen? Brav dich was vermessen?
> Dem Feinde vorgespiegelt dies und das?
> Mit Lug and Trug verkehrt? Ei ja, ich weiß.   (1716–20)

(Ah, my daredevil. My gallant faithful boy! Here is my hand! No, do not kiss it, press it, like this. Well, have you told some good lies? played a few good tricks? misled the enemy with this and that? practiced falsehood and deceit? Ah yes, I know.)

Nevertheless, this does not necessarily signal a revision of his ethical position, only an acknowledgment that ordinary mortals should not be harshly judged if they fall short of its absolute standards. At the close, the bishop turns sadly from the world of deceit to the realm of eternal truth associated with his own spiritual calling. In the bishop's final attitude to Leon we may see once again an expression of the ambivalent relationship between an ideal that is all too perfect, impracticable, and essentially other-worldly and the imperfect, yet attractive forces of life. This final scene suggests Grillparzer's own regret at the vanishing ideal of the bishop, yet also his own acceptance of its limitations, and his recognition that Leon's methods have brought success and happiness, in spite of being ethically questionable.

Grillparzer would have had every justification is assuming that his positive presentation of Leon's dubious maneuvers would have appealed to the Viennese fun-loving audience. And so it might have, but for the fact that Grillparzer chose to have his comedy performed where *Der Traum ein Leben* had found favor, in the Burgtheater itself. There were several aspects of the comedy that would have had a strong appeal in the popular suburban theater, but that found little favor with some of the more sophisticated and conservative elements in the Burgtheater audience. In the early stages of the play, for example, there is humor in Leon's refreshingly honest and cheeky exchange with his master, the bishop, in his down-to-earth and occasionally witty language. But later this kind of linguistic or situational comedy gives way to blatant slapstick, such as when the bridge collapses under Galomir, who is vainly pursuing the fleeing Leon and Atalus. Galomir himself is a cretinous character, designed to represent the primitive stupidity of the barbarians, which Grillparzer exaggerates by using animal-like grunts and monosyllables. Grillparzer's realism has here degenerated into grotesque caricature, hardly the most subtle form of comedy. Again, Leon is one of Grillparzer's most sympathetically drawn characters, and with his sunny disposition, naive ingenuity, and commonsense approach to the practicalities of life, he is clearly designed to appeal to the popular audience. But he is also a lowly servant, and the people he constantly appears to outwit are his masters—situations which the insecure aristocrats only a decade away from 1848 might have found potentially dangerous. In particular, Leon makes Count Kattwald look ridiculous, never more so than in the scene in which he steals the key to the outer gate from Kattwald's bedside. When Kattwald awakens, Leon throws the key away, confesses both to the theft and to this ruse, and then proceeds to look for the key under Kattwald's own foot! The portrayal of Atalus, too, was hardly flattering to the Viennese upper classes. He cooperates only reluctantly with Leon's escape plans, primarily for reasons of snobbishness, and Leon surpasses him both in native wit and personal charm. In the portraits of Kattwald and Atalus we see Grillparzer's potential for social and political satire. Another potentially appealing ingredient of the play was the theme of the contrast between the civilized French and the uncultured barbarians east of the Rhine, which might have suggested to the Viennese audience their own presumed cultural superiority over their German neighbors. But again, the choice of a mere kitchen-boy with his culinary skills as the embodiment of civilization, while the barbarians were portrayed as his aristocratic masters, was alarming in its social implications. Viewed in this light, it is understandable why the comedy was so badly received by those sections of the Burgtheater audience that had readily accepted the cosy Biedermeier moral of *Der Traum ein Leben.*

But if the aristocrats in the audience found the play disagreeably controversial, the less sophisticated elements who were expecting a rollicking comedy were disappointed for different reasons. True, there is comedy, slapstick even, but the play's main appeal is provided by the love theme, the relationship which develops between Leon and Kattwald's daughter Edrita, and which is one of Grillparzer's most touching creations. In two senses this too furnishes the play with good stock comedy material, for Edrita turns to Leon as a more attractive alternative to her father's choice for her, the impossible Galomir, and then at the play's conclusion we rejoice that Leon has returned with Edrita even more than over the safe return of Atalus. But the motif is also treated with some subtlety and is carefully interwoven with the intellectual problem of expediency and absolute truth. This may have made the play intellectually more challenging for some, but also have obscured some of its more immediate comic appeal for others. In attempting to please two contrasting groups in his audience, Grillparzer has been less successful than in *Der Traum ein Leben.*

The relationship between Leon and Edrita develops naturally from their first encounter, when Leon appeals to the artless and forthright barbarian maiden with his own openness and frankness. Thereafter, the love affair makes an important contribution to Leon's success, for unbeknown to him, Edrita lends him vital assistance during the episode in which he attempts to steal the key. After the comic scene which ensues when Kattwald awakens to catch Leon in the very act, Leon eventually discovers the key which he required, sitting conveniently in its own lock. He naturally assumes that some miracle has occurred, but Edrita reveals that it is no angel who has intervened, but her own very real human self. Leon's piece of subterfuge would not have sufficed in itself to ensure success, any more than a wholehearted adherence to the spirit of the bishop's ethic. The miracle of true love is the vital factor here. At this point, however, problems arise. As Edrita watches his plans for escape, she regrets that he is thereby betraying the image that she has formed of him. "Though you have always spoken the truth, I feel nevertheless that you have deceived me," she says accusingly, placing her hand on her heart as she does so (1137f.). Out of the intellectual problem of the relationship between absolute truth and expediency has emerged an emotional issue, emphasized here by Edrita's gesture. [12] Yet, despite her disappointment in him, Edrita now goes even further in her alliance with Leon, by joining him and Atalus in flight. To some extent her action is prompted by her need to escape a wrathful father, even by an idealistic desire to become a Christian, but her prime motive derives, as she later intimates to the bishop, from her feelings for Leon, even though she is not conscious of this fact at the actual moment of decision (1742f.). Edrita makes an intuitive leap in the dark, and her instincts do not play her false, for the opening scene, in which Leon takes the bishop to task for his miserliness, shows that by *nature* Leon is truly the honest and open fellow who first attracted her. His deceitful behavior, which made Edrita temporarily doubt the reliability of her feelings, may be attributed simply to the practical demands of his mission. In the final analysis, then, it is Leon's nature and Edrita's intuitive response to him that win the day.

But just as Edrita momentarily has second thoughts about Leon, Leon, for his part, is prepared to sacrifice his feelings in pursuit of a successful conclusion to his mission. When Edrita begs him to remain at her father's house for her own sake, he has to refuse, and then when she follows him in flight he is most reluctant to permit her to accompany him, lest he incur the bishop's displeasure over this unplanned piece of "robbery." By the time they reach safety he has virtually disclaimed her, but eventually his true feelings gain the upper hand.

If the play's central events do not represent a victory for truth in the
absolute sense of the bishop's ethic, neither do they necessarily
denote the supremacy of expediency and deception. Truth has won a
victory here in a form radically different from that originally required
by the bishop, not truth in the narrow and literal sense of "not telling
lies," but truth in the broader sense of the true feelings of the human
heart. The power of love asserts itself as a theme of ever increasing
importance, first as a factor motivating Edrita's behavior, and then as
a phenomenon sufficiently valuable in itself to provide the play with
its satisfying conclusion. In the treatment of its initial theme, *Weh
dem, der lügt!* is a more problematic play than *Der Traum ein Leben.*
No explicit moral emerges; indeed, the "moral" of the title is neither
upheld nor refuted by events, and a new theme emerges. Yet at the
same time it is Grillparzer's most cheerful work, the work in which
the realm of human emotions is presented most sympathetically and
in its most innocent light.

The plays of Grillparzer's middle years present two interestingly
contrasting pairs, the harrowing tragedies of *Ein treuer Diener* and
Des Meeres und der Liebe Wellen being followed by the relatively
happier conclusions of *Der Traum ein Leben* and *Weh dem, der lügt!*
To some extent this development is due to Grillparzer's readoption of
more popular dramatic forms, but it also reflects his own gradual
emergence from the acute despondency of the 1820s. There is also
evidence of a greater tolerance of his fellow beings and of a growing
sympathy for human passions, though in this respect *Der Traum ein
Leben* provides something of a throwback to an earlier attitude. At
the same time there are signs of an increasing distrust for ideals,
which are presented as either inhumane or impractical. These ideals
or values vary from play to play, but we can perceive in these plays a
dichotomy which appeared first in *Sappho:* the dichotomy of natural
inclinations and some kind of principle, whether political, religious,
or ethical, which is essentially restrictive. These plays are not necessarily plays of ideas, but they do present values, or modes of existence, and so have invited interpretations of a philosophical kind.
They also provide an illustration of Grillparzer's tendency to base his
works on a fundamental dualism of opposing realms, embodying on
one hand an existence sustained by the urges of ambition or love, on
the other one involving a withdrawal from participation in the normal
forces of life. In this respect, *Der Traum ein Leben* also possesses an
underlying structure of this kind, for the Biedermeier ideal which is
posed there involves a stifling of inclinations, a retreat in resignation

from the outside world and a sacrifice of fulfillment and wholeness of being. It is characteristic of Grillparzer that the values or modes of life which he depicts are never seen as totally satisfactory or fulfilling, whether they embody a high ideal whose demands are intolerable, or natural inclinations which, however sympathetically they may be presented, may bring guilt or danger. To some extent, this dualism reflects aspects of Grillparzer's own personal experience, but his particularly skeptical treatment of it is also suggestive of an awareness, which he shared with many of his nineteenth-century contemporaries, that the eighteenth-century Goethean ideal of the education and fulfillment of the human personality in its totality, was but a lost ideal of the past.

CHAPTER 4

Poetry and Prose

I *Poetry*

I T IS ostensibly one of the more puzzling facts of literary history
that whereas Grillparzer enjoys considerable stature as a
dramatist, as a lyric poet he ranks only as a minor figure. Not that he is
entirely unknown as a poet, for individual lines have become im-
mortalized, such as "In your camp is Austria," which offered encouragement to Fieldmarshal Radetzky in whose imperial army
Grillparzer saw the salvation of his fatherland during the troubles of
1848, and his description of Vienna as "a Capua of minds," referring to
its relaxing atmosphere, so lacking in intellectual stimulus. But in
both cases it is the thought behind the words that is striking, not the
poetic formulation itself, and it is the reflective tone of his poems that
is generally held to be the reason for their failure to achieve lasting
recognition. As a poet Grillparzer has been seen as a descendant of
the Rationalist tradition of the eighteenth century, writing under the
influence of figures of the Enlightenment such as Christian Gellert
and Martin Wieland, a tradition that strongly persisted in Austria in
Grillparzer's lifetime.

The volume and range of Grillparzer's poetry is impressive. In his
early period—up to the early 1820s—there are his youthful attempts
at writing nature poetry such as "Der Abend" [Evening, 1806],
reminiscent of the Anacreontic lyrics of Ewald von Kleist, and ballads
which owe an obvious debt to Schiller. Further eighteenth-century
influence can be detected in a leaning toward didactic poems, for
example, fables such as "Die beiden Hunde" [The Two Dogs, 1806].
But there are also several more subjective lyrics such as "An Ovid"
(1812), expressing his suicidal despair at being left so little time to
compose poetry, and "Abschied von Gastein" [Farewell to Gastein,
1818], which is a moving statement on the fate of the creative artist,
communicating fragments of his own joyless life to his readers.

Most of Grillparzer's subjective lyrics were written during his most
fruitful period between 1820 and 1836, and provide an intimate

record of his personal problems and a fascinating supplement to his diaries. "Incubus" (1821) is an expression of the gloom that overcame him following the failure of *Das goldene Vlieβ*, while "Kaiphas, Kaiphas, Sanchedrin" (1823) is a bitter, almost blasphemous poem comparing his failure to obtain promotion with Christ's crucifixion. "Der Halbmond glänzet am Himmel" [The Crescent Moon Shines in the Sky, 1827] is a statement on the contradictions in his personality and his failure to taste fully either the ordinary joys of life or success as an artist. But most of Grillparzer's confessional lyrics relate to his love life. There are attempts to capture the most striking features of the various women in his life. Kathi Fröhlich's dark eyes in "Allgegen-wart" [Omnipresence, 1821], the latent beauty of the youthful Marie, who is likened in "Rangstreit" [Fight for Status, 1825] to a rose hiding its fullest bloom among a labyrinth of leaves, and the innocent charm of Heloise Hoechner in "Begegnung" [Meeting, 1830]. Some of these lyrics have a conciseness which belies the complexity of Grillparzer's emotional situation. For example, in "Willst du, ich soll Hütten bauen?" [Do You Want Me to Settle Down?, 1827] he explains his persistent refusal to commit himself to marriage in the deceptively simple terms of a desire to fulfill himself through experience in the world.

The opening stanza of "Allgegenwart" [Omnipresence] suggests an ability to write free rhythms with the linguistic inventiveness and spontaneous ease of the young Goethe:

> Wo ich bin, fern und nah,
> Stehen zwei Augen da,
> Dunkelhell,
> Blitzesschnell,
> Schimmernd wie Felsenquell,
> Schattenumkränzt.

(Wherever I am, near or far away, there are two eyes, dark-bright, lightning-fast, gleaming like a mountain spring, adorned with shadows.)

But the second stanza introduces an ingenious "idea." The power of Kathi's eyes is likened to that of the sun, which for anyone who has been looking straight into it, still appears as two little black dots in the mind's eye, even when he has closed his eyes. A metaphor conceived with equal ingenuity, but more elaborately developed, is used in "Das Spiegelbild" [The Reflection] to represent Charlotte after Grillparzer ended his affair with her in 1821. She is seen as the still water of a well in which Grillparzer sees his reflection, and who thus contains within her the longing of his heart. Yet in the water, too, he sees the reflection of her husband, his cousin and friend, to whom she has, after all, remained faithful. How could Grillparzer have built his hopes on something so insubstantial as water?! This imagery has a clever, almost intellectual quality, and is too obviously contrived. On the other hand, when Grillparzer wrote in a simpler vein, his language could be banal, as in his final poem to Marie in 1831:

> Ich weiß ein Haar, das ist so schwarz,
> Ich weiß ein Aug, das ist so groß,
> Ich weiß ein Herz, das ist so gut,
> Und einen Mund, der spricht so süß.

(I know hair that is so black, I know an eye that is so big, I know a heart that is so good, and a mouth that speaks so sweetly.)

This mixture of cleverness and banality partly accounts for his lack of success as a lyric-poet.

Yet during this same period Grillparzer also wrote a series of more impressive lyrics which he published in 1835 as a cycle entitled *Tristia ex Ponto*. The *Tristia* were prompted by Grillparzer's inner crisis of 1826 and represent an attempt to come to terms with the major problem, which he faced in the years immediately following, the recurrent elusiveness of artistic inspiration. The main theme of the *Tristia* is announced in the first poem, "Böse Stunde" [Evil Hour], in which the poet states his intention of seeking inspiration through real-life experience. Yet the experiences described in the poems which follow scarcely offer any comfort. They cause him only pain, and the prevailing mood of the cycle is one of gloom. His attempt to find some stimulus in his journey to Germany described in "Reiselust" [Desire for Travel] ends with the humiliating encounter with Goethe. When he turns to Marie, he tells us in "Verwünschung" [Curse] that he finds in her a combination of physical beauty and an evil heart, qualities possessed by the angel of death, that fill him with both ecstasy and horror:

> Und so, gemischt aus Wonne und aus Grauen,
> Stehst du, ein Todesengel, neben mir,
> Ein Engel zwar, doch auch ein Tod zu schauen,
> Und wer da lebt, der hüte sich vor dir.

(And so, a mixture of delight and horror, you stand beside me like an angel of death, an angel indeed, yet to look at you is death, and anyone who lives near you must beware of you.)

Again we see a tendency to think out consciously the imagery of his poetry, to use his reason to convey the import of his passions.[1] That he is, on the other hand, capable of a more immediate expression of emotion can be seen in the cri-de-coeur which ends "Noch einmal in Gastein" [In Gastein again], in which he contrasts his broken mental state of 1831 with the optimism he felt on his visit there ten years previously:

> Nun bin ich müd, gestört, entzweit,
> Nur Mauern läßt die Bergwand mir gewahren,
> O, eine ganze Ewigkeit
> Liegt in dem Raum von zehen Jahren!

(Now I am tired, disturbed, divided in myself. On the mountain face I can only see walls. Oh, what an eternity there is in the space of ten years!)

Similarly, in the long autobiographical poem *Jugenderinnerungen im Grünen* [Memories of Youth in the Countryside] in which he sums up the disappointments of his life and describes, in particular, the agonizing course of his relationship with Kathi, he can produce the spontaneous cry: "Oh blessed feeling of those early days, why were you no more than a dream?" in the midst of the more sober-sounding, carefully reasoned account. This poem provides an appropriate background to the pessimistic themes of his tragedies, conveying Grillparzer's own impression that everything that he had touched in life had gone sour, and ending on a note of despairing disillusionment. At the conclusion of the cycle, however, Grillparzer suddenly perceives the link between his unhappy experiences and the initial theme of the pursuit of artistic inspiration. In the penultimate poem "Freundeswort" [Message of a Friend] he tells Bauernfeld that his poetry can amount to nothing more than an outburst of pain, written with the blood of his own wounds, after which he feels in "Schluß-wort" [Conclusion] that his despair has passed and his suffering has been put behind him like a dream. In other words, although the lesson of the *Tristia* is that experience itself will bring pain, Grillparzer's experiences have indeed brought him the desired inspiration to write. Moreover, the act of creation, the translation of his suffering into poetry, may itself bring relief. The concluding lines of the cycle represent, therefore, one of the few occasions on which Grillparzer was able to reconcile the opposing principles of art and life, and to recognize that the latter could serve the requirements of the former.

As Grillparzer grew older, his personal lyrics grew rarer, and a new form, the political poem, predominated during his final creative period. Grillparzer had already given evidence of his keen interest in contemporary affairs in a number of poems, but until the 1830s his technique had been allusive rather than explicit. As it was, the political implications of "Campo Vaccino" (1819) had given considerable offense, so that in the 1820s he restricted himself to a few brief poems whose political relevance was barely discernible. In "Jagd im Winter" [Winter Hunt, 1826], for example, he cleverly suggests that in urging the hunter to defy the cold of winter, he is really challenging poets like himself to defy the harshness of police censorship. Then in 1831 came two poems with more outspoken political sentiments, "Klosterszene" [Monastery Scene] and "Warschau" [Warsaw]. The first, ostensibly about Charles V, contains a strong attack on the repression of freedom, which clearly refers to the contemporary situation in Austria, and which caused the poem to be banned. The second is a revolutionary poem which deplores the crushing of the Polish insurrection by Russian troops and castigates the European powers for failing to intervene. This he did not even attempt to publish.

Following his journey to France and England in 1836, he wrote a large number of political poems. Most of these remained unpublished, at least until after 1848, and although they are far less extreme than those written by many of his more radical contemporaries, they do reflect the moderate liberal views that he held during these years. Many of them are addressed to prominent political figures such as Metternich, whose financial policies he satirized in 1836 in "Für unser Glück" [For our Happiness], and Frederick William IV, whom he urged in 1841 in "Warnung" [Warning] to honor his promise to grant Prussia a constitution. Some poems provide a more extended treatment of the general political situation. "Des Kaisers Bildsäule" [The Emperor's Statue, 1837] presents the complaints of the statue of Joseph II against the current age, which has abandoned his reformist principles and civilized humanitarian ideals; "Vorzeichen" [Portent, January 1848] is an analysis of the pre-revolutionary situation in Austria, in which his hostility toward the regime is matched by his fears of the coming upheaval.

Such poems amount to a personal commentary on this momentous period in Austria's history and are primarily of historical value. Yet Grillparzer's political verses deserve a more prominent place in the literature of the Vormärz than they are usually accorded. The following stanza of "Vorzeichen" provides a typical example of his hard-hitting style, as he urges the members of the government to adopt further repressive measures in the face of the people's demands for reforms, only to reveal his own scorn for this policy through the ironic twist of the last line:

> Klagt euch das Denken seiner Freiheit Schranken,
> —Ruft einen Büttel, der noch engre gibt!
> Der Krone Vorrecht seien die Gedanken,
> Ein Vorrecht, das man etwa sparsam übt.

(If you complain of [the people's] thoughts about the limitations on freedom,—send for a bailiff who will provide still harsher measures! Let thoughts be the privilege of the crown, a privilege which is exercised somewhat rarely.)

Frequently Grillparzer's verse has a distinctly witty and satirical flavor, and its lightly mocking tone bears comparison with that evoked in the political satires of Austria's foremost political poet of the time, Anastasius Grün, and of Heinrich Heine, whom Grillparzer met while in Paris in 1836.

The same kind of acumen and wit is to be found in the innumerable epigrams and aphorisms that Grillparzer penned during his later years. Many of these amount to little more than intellectual word-games or wise offerings for the *Stammbuch* ("family album") of some acquaintance or admirer, but some provide sharp comments on contemporary issues, both political and cultural. They range, for example, from his protestation in 1843 that so many of his countrymen have been spiritually enslaved through recruitment into the imperial army, to his expression of scorn for the students of 1848, who have abandoned their studies to destroy their fatherland; from his criticism of contemporary poets generally, who are pregnant with works of genius, but who rarely give birth, to specific attacks on the poets Ludwig Uhland and Ludwig Tieck, and the philosophers Schelling and Hegel. Frequently he takes refuge in sardonic wit and a half-amused, phlegmatic resignation:

Preßfreiheit steht denn oben an,
Wo—welch absurdes Treiben!—
Das halbe Land nicht lesen kann,
Das andre nicht schreiben.

(Freedom of the Press should suit those up above, where—what absurd
goings on!—half the country can't read, the other half can't write.)

On the other hand, he can also express concisely and pointedly his
genuine concern at what he sees as an inexorable regression from the
cultural values of the eighteenth century to a future barbarism: "Der
Weg der neuen Bildung geht / Von Humanität / Durch Nationalität /
Zur Bestialität" (The path of modern culture leads from humanity,
through nationalism, to bestiality.)

Finally, we may mention the large number of occasional poems,
whose chief merit is that they offer a record and impression of cultural
life in the Vienna of the Vormärz. The least interesting commemorate
births, marriages, deaths, and anniversaries of friends, relatives, and
public figures. Some were to be recited or sung on public occasions,
such as the opening of the new concert-hall for the Gesellschaft der
Musikfreunde. Others are addressed to friends such as Schreyvogel,
the Pichler family, Count Stadion, or Count Auersperg. There are
also poems recording performances by Liszt, Clara Schumann, and
Rossini, assessments of the work of Beethoven and Schubert, a
description of Kathi Fröhlich singing, accompanied by Schubert at
the piano. In that these poems are drawn from and relate essentially
to Grillparzer's own experience and environment, they are truly
zeitbedingt, a quality which Ernst Alker perceives in much of
Grillparzer's poetry, and to which he partly attributes Grillparzer's
lack of recognition.[2] In the history of German poetry Grillparzer is an
isolated figure, writing essentially of his own life and times. Though
his personal lyrics occasionally possess the elegiac tone of his compat-
riot Lenau, and his political poetry the flavor of Heine, he is associated with no particular literary movement. He avoided the subjective extravagances of some of the early German Romantics, did not
share the Romantic love for the folksong, was too moderate in his
views for the majority of the political poets of the Vormärz, and
apparently lacked the sensitivity to the world of nature associated
with the late Romantics and the Poetic Realists.

II Das Kloster bei Sendomir

In view of the fact that Grillparzer regarded poetry so much more highly than prose, it is more surprising that he should have written creatively in prose at all, than that he should have made only two contributions to the most popular genre of the nineteenth century in Germany, the shorter prose narrative. Grillparzer's two short stories, *Das Kloster bei Sendomir* and *Der arme Spielmann*, are dissimilar in content and atmosphere, and have also had markedly contrasting receptions. The former, published in 1827, has been generally regarded as a minor work and has received scant critical attention, but the latter, published in 1847, has been the subject of numerous critical studies, and has been acclaimed as one of the masterpieces in the history of the German *Novelle*. Both works are deeply rooted in Grillparzer's personal experience, treating respectively two of the dominant passions of his life, namely, love and devotion to his art. The autobiographical element is here even more than usually prominent, and it has been seen as the principal reason for Grillparzer's retreat in these two particular cases into the more protective form of prose narrative.[3]

With the sensational and improbable character of its subject-matter, its atmosphere of tension and mystery, its lack of detailed characterization, and its violent, melodramatic conclusion, *Das Kloster bei Sendomir* [The Monastery of Sendomir] recalls aspects of Romantic horror literature, and Kleistian and Hoffmannesque qualities have been detected in it, both stylistic and atmospheric. Grillparzer had thus returned to the kind of material that had produced *Die Ahnfrau*, and to a genre that had really run its course. Yet it is a powerful story of dark passions and violence, treating the themes of adultery and murder, and presents a disturbing picture of an ill-fated marriage.

The story is narrated by a mysterious monk, who turns out to be the central character Starschensky, a Polish count who is lured into marrying a woman of voluptuous beauty called Elga, who accosts him at night on the streets of Warsaw. Though Elga is no prostitute in the technical sense, but the daughter of an impoverished nobleman, she ensnares Starschensky, who duly marries her and rescues her father from his precarious financial position. The couple settle down on Starschensky's estate and a daughter is born, but it is not long before their domestic harmony is disturbed. There are reports that a dark

figure has been visiting the house at night, and Starschensky finds
among Elga's possessions a portrait of her cousin Oginsky, which
bears a strong resemblance to the child. The suspicious Starschensky
returns to Warsaw, and inquiries reveal that Elga and Oginsky did
indeed have a previous love affair. Later he reappears at home
accompanied by a hooded figure whom he locks in a disused tower on
the estate. In the final melodramatic scene Starschensky reveals to
Elga that the figure is Oginsky himself, who has confessed to the
paternity of the child. Oginsky flees, but Starschensky cuts Elga
down with his sword and sets fire to the tower. Later he establishes a
monastery near the site, becomes a monk, and does nightly penance
for his monstrous crime.

Conceived as early as 1820, *Das Kloster* was based originally on
Grillparzer's relationship with Charlotte, Oginsky's flight and
Starschensky's violent revenge apparently representing Grillparzer's
judgment on his own adultery with his cousin's wife. Yet the story was
largely written in 1825, when Grillparzer had fallen under the spell of
Marie and was already harboring suspicions about her character.
Moreover, it is told from the viewpoint of the deceived Starschensky,
rather than from that of the treacherous Oginsky, who remains a
shadowy figure. Thus, as Douglas Yates has pointed out, the situation
anticipates with uncanny accuracy Grillparzer's circumstances in
1826, when he felt himself betrayed by his friend Daffinger, who
turned out to be the father of Marie's child.

Starschensky's story is narrated by himself, but in the third person
so that he achieves a degree of objectivity about his own fate. His
story is presented with sympathy, but also critically. Starschensky
comes to Warsaw as an "innocent," having led a solitary existence and
having had little contact with women, but this was due to his own love
of independence and isolation. Thus he is particularly susceptible to
Elga's charms, as she virtually seduces him into marrying her.[4] She
takes the initiative in their physical relations, then tantalizes him by
keeping him at a distance. When they are married, she indulges in a
life of expensive pleasure-seeking. Yet Starschensky is still blissfully
happy with her, blinded by passion, a victim both of his own naiveté
and of this dangerously alluring creature. But though she is in some
ways a forerunner of the cocquettish Rahel of *Die Jüdin von Toledo*,
no character in Grillparzer's work is reduced to such a level of cynical
inhumanity as is Elga in the final nightmarish scene. This scene
brings the work closest to some of Kleist's stories, when Starschensky
threatens Elga with death, but indicates that he will spare her if she

will kill the child. Elga at first protests, but soon she agrees in order to save her own life. But, before she can murder the child, Starschensky reveals that this was a trick, a test of her humanity, which she has failed, so he kills her nevertheless. In Elga the instinct for self-preservation has outweighed the instinct of maternal love; in Starschensky reason has become tainted with jealous passion, and the result is a cruelly difficult test of Elga's integrity, followed by brutal revenge. Perhaps a Kleistian Elga would have made an intuitive leap in the dark and perceived the meaning of Starschensky's test, but in Grillparzer's story there is no such salvation for the characters.

Just as Starschensky has been able to objectify his story through the medium of third-person narrative, so too has Grillparzer, through Starschensky, presented his own situation at an even greater distance. He has also exaggerated and distorted his experiences, translating his own pain, self-criticism, and, above all, his fears concerning both the nature of Marie and his own potential reaction, into a fictional situation.

III   Der arme Spielmann

Grillparzer's second prose work, *Der arme Spielmann* [The Poor Musician], was begun in 1831, but not completed until about 1842. It is a more mature work than *Das Kloster*, but again a major problem concerns the relationship between author and subject, and the story has alarming implications for Grillparzer's misgivings concerning the value of his own art. The most immediately striking feature of the work is the framework which has been constructed round the central story of the musician. This takes up over a third of the work and is more elaborate than that used in his previous story. Like Starschensky, the musician gives his own account of himself, though here in the more usual form of first-person narrative. Yet Grillparzer again distances himself from his subject, in this case by interposing between reader and musician a narrator, a dramatist like himself, as though to discourage any assumption that the musician is simply a projection of Grillparzer's own self.

The narrator first notices the musician playing his violin to the crowds near the Augarten on the occasion of a popular festival, and the two have a brief conversation. Later that evening he listens to him from the street below as he plays in his room in the Leopoldstadt. But the musician's story is not told until the narrator actually visits him a few days later. Through the narrator's eagerness to get to know him

Grillparzer convinces us that he is a case worth investigating. The impression received is that of an eccentric curiosity, for there is a striking element of incongruity in the musician's appearance and behavior. He stands alongside a group of beggar musicians, yet his dress and manner suggest a genteel and educated background, and he is serenely oblivious to his lowly surroundings. But his music is the most remarkable aspect of him. He is engrossed in his performance, which gives him obvious pleasure, and the sheet music on the stand before him suggests a more professional approach than that taken by the majority of his kind. Indeed, he tells the narrator that he practices daily difficult compositions by the best composers. Yet what he produces is a disconnected sequence of sounds without melody or rhythm, a confusion unrecognizable as belonging to any particular piece of music and which is even painful to the ear.

Thus far the musician has remained a mystery to the narrator and it is only by having him tell his own story that he can get close to the truth about him.[5] As suggested by his appearance, the musician has indeed known better days, and his story constitutes a pathetic record of failure. Dull and painstakingly slow at his lessons, he becomes estranged from his father, who is an influential and ambitious man, and who obviously tries to forget his son's existence. He is given a menial copying job in the chancellery, and at home he leads a narrow and solitary life. When his father dies, he unexpectedly finds himself a rich man, but he imprudently entrusts his wealth to a rogue and is quickly ruined. This apparently empty and fruitless life is enriched by one engrossing experience, from which springs his passion for music. One evening he hears a girl in the courtyard below his room sing a song which entrances him, and which he finds he can play on the violin, an instrument he has not touched since childhood. The singer is a grocer's daughter, Barbara, and with timidity and embarrassment he seeks her acquaintance, initially to obtain the score of the song. She treats him with disdain, and when he visits her father's shop she ignores him. But, with the encouragement of her father, the visit is repeated, and gradually she begins to tolerate him. She even seems not to exclude the possibility of marriage when she advises him to take a shop, which she will help him run. Only when his financial ruin is discovered does she dismiss him, to marry a butcher whose proposal she had hitherto rejected. As for the musician, he is left to play his music and to give lessons to Barbara's children.

While the facts of the musician's story partly satisfy the narrator's curiosity, the story itself raises fundamental questions concerning our assessment of the man and his "music." He emerges from the story as a pathetic and occasionally absurd character, but though he is outwardly incompetent, there is no doubting either the honesty of his intentions or his moral integrity. In his office-job he works so slowly that he is thought to be lazy, yet this is because he is a perfectionist. His love for his father is such that instead of protesting against the harsh treatment that he suffers, he feels he should apologize for causing his father trouble. He allows himself to be cheated of his wealth, never imagining that not all possess the same honesty as himself. He has a decency that is occasionally misplaced or exaggerated, and that is literally too good for the world in which he lives. That his moral standards are not those of his fellowmen is suggested by the symbolic chalk line that he draws across the room to separate his own territory from that of the other lodgers. The order and cleanliness of his sector contrast with the disorder and dirt of theirs, but it is significant that whereas he observes the division, they do not. It is a one-sided and futile arrangement, from which he cannot profit in any practical sense, and there is a clear distinction between his interpretation of the situation and actuality. He is one of life's innocents, lacking the practical fiber and judgment necessary for survival.

Eventually it is his lack of judgment that leads to his death, which occurs about a year after the musician's narration of his story, and which conveniently completes the framework and rounds off the work. It is set in February 1830, at the time of Vienna's great flood, and the Leopoldstadt is a major disaster area. Fearing for the musician's welfare, the narrator returns there to offer him assistance, only to discover that he has perished. He had behaved heroically, rescuing children from the flood, but it was not this that killed him. He died of a cold caught when he had gone back in foolhardy fashion to save his landlord's tax returns. Both actions were undertaken in the same spirit of selfless generosity, but in the exercise of his virtue he failed to discriminate between a matter of life and death and a triviality.[6]

The musician's inadequacies are most cruelly exposed in his relationship with Barbara. When they first become acquainted in the chancellery, where she sells refreshments, she asks for a piece of paper on which to place her cakes, a casual request, but he goes to ridiculous lengths to please her. Instead of simply taking a piece from the office, which he dare not do, he fetches a whole quire of paper from his home a few days later, a response which is well-meaning and which serves to further the acquaintanceship, but which at face value is absurdly inappropriate. From the reader's viewpoint the relationship seems a particularly humiliating one for the musician, for Barbara scolds him incessantly for his clumsiness and general ineptitude, showing us exactly what marriage to her would have been like for him. Yet the reader can detect in Barbara signs of genuine affection for him. When they part, she is emotionally distressed, and at the close of the work she is seen weeping over his memory. Clearly she senses something of value in his nature and character, yet at the same time she is exasperated that he is so weak, gullible, impractical, and effeminate. The musician is both saint and fool, a paradox which is reflected in the ambivalence of Barbara's feelings toward him.

It is possible that Grillparzer is offering through his presentation of the musician's unhappy fate a comment on the unscrupulous harshness of his own materialistic world, and we can despair that one so pure in soul becomes an outcast and beggar. The implication is that sterner qualities are required for survival in an unsympathetic world, qualities which the musician does not possess. Yet if he did possess them, he would lose something of his essential nobility. A similarly ironic combination of nobility of character and impracticality has been observed in the portraits of Bancbanus and Bishop Gregor, but in *Der arme Spielmann* greater emphasis is placed on the hero's inadequacies. He has been justly identified as one of the first true anti-heroes of nineteenth-century literature. One incident in particular, which stands at the center of the story, suggests that the blame for his failure rests more with his own character and personality than with society. This occurs at the climax of his relationship with Barbara when he attempts to embrace her for the only time. Her response is to strike him hard on the face, but then to kiss him lightly on the cheek. She then flees from him, and as she shuts the glass door in his face, he returns her kiss by pressing his lips passionately against the glass. The emotions that prompt Barbara's contradictory actions here are clearly identifiable. The blow represents a spontaneous reaction, her genuine anger at what she regards as an impertinence. Her kiss is only a fleeting gesture of remorse, in no sense an expression of love. Yet the musician is thrown into ecstasies by the blow, and the memory of the kiss still brings tears to his eyes. His reaction is wholly inappropriate, for he invests in each of her actions a significance that is out of all proportion with reality. The gulf between reality and his own private view is symbolized by the glass which separates him and Barbara and in his ineffectual and grotesquely ridiculous attempt at a kiss. The incident both highlights his inadequacies as a man and suggests a profound division between himself and his fellow beings.

The musician's feelings for Barbara in themselves are also somewhat problematic. That this is no simple love story is suggested by the
absence of any confession of love on his part. Nor is there any
indication that he finds Barbara beautiful. Indeed, his colleagues find
her pock-marked and generally unattractive, an opinion which he
does not dispute. What does attract him is her song. It is the song that
he finds beautiful, and it is his desire to possess the score of it that
leads him to Barbara's home. It is when he finds her singing it that he
attempts to embrace her; it is the song that he teaches to her elder
child, that he plays after concluding his story, and that has retained its
beauty for him over the years. The song thus possesses a unique
significance for him and exercises over him a frightening demonic
power. On the other hand, it affords him an ecstatic pleasure and is
the only piece of music that he can play with any success. Indeed, he
feels divinely inspired when he first plays it; it surpasses Bach and
Mozart and provides access to God. When he dies, he smiles, as
though he can hear something beautiful far away. It is thus arguable
that his music has brought him close to "the divine source of truth and
beauty,"[7] providing his life with spiritual and aesthetic riches which it
would otherwise have lacked, and which transcend the ephemeral
values of reality.

Yet if the musician's ears are attuned to some loftier ideal realm, he
is unable to demonstrate this, for in that it fails to communicate
anything of the feeling that has inspired the performer, his music is
artistically worthless. The pleasure that he finds in his song is entirely
private, for both to the narrator and to Barbara it sounds just like any
ordinary popular song. Moreover, although he claims to have a
serious artistic mission, he is totally unsuccessful in performance.
Because he lacks the ability to communicate, to "perform" the ecstasy
he feels, value cannot be ascribed to it in any absolute sense.[8] *Der
arme Spielmann* underlines the fact that the power of the artist's
vision is without value for others if it is not translated into intelligible
art. As Grillparzer himself insisted, the basis of every art is
craftsmanship, and any would-be artist who does not possess this
quality is an incompetent, a *Stümper* (SB I, 14, 73). The musician's
aesthetic experience may have significance for himself, but it is for his
own pleasure alone. His devotion to his art and the evidence of the
ecstasy that he derives from this are indicative of the capacity of art for
the enrichment of life, but in that his art takes him into a private
world which he cannot share with others, it is sterile. The gulf
between the musician and reality, which exists in any case because of

his shortcomings as a human being, is accentuated by the privacy of his art. Thus, although he has given his own subjective account of his story, we have still not got to the bottom of the mystery, for his deepest secret, the pleasure which he takes in his music, has remained impenetrable.

It is not without significance that *Der arme Spielmann* was completed at a time when Grillparzer's doubts as to the validity of his own art had reached a critical stage. The autobiographical element in this story is strong, and in an exaggerated and distorted fashion the portrait of the musician does reflect Grillparzer's relationship with his father, with Kathi Fröhlich, his own devotion to his art, and his tortured self-doubts both as man and artist.[9] If his earlier artist-figure Sappho also expressed Grillparzer's awareness of the gulf separating the artist from life, at least the value of her art was not questioned. But the value of the musician's art *is* questioned, and precisely because, in the true sense of the word, he is no artist. At most, he can represent Grillparzer's deepest fears as to the image that he himself might present to his unappreciative public. He is a distortion of the *unsuccessful* artist, and a warning of the dangers of an over-subjective, Romantic attitude to art. But he is also a forerunner of some of the sickly and decadent artist-figures of Thomas Mann, such as Detlev Spinell of *Tristan*, who enjoys the most exquisite, but uncommunicable private aesthetic experiences. In Grillparzer's musician's devotion to his song we may see an anticipation of the exclusive aestheticism and rarefied idealism that was to become such a cult at the turn of the century.

CHAPTER 5

Politics and the Final Tragedies

I Politics

G RILLPARZER'S last three tragedies have a strongly political flavor, reflecting Grillparzer's own growing political consciousness in the 1840s. These three plays he withheld from publication in his lifetime, and because they were, for the most part, not written with the constraints of censorship in mind, they are thought to offer a more honest expression of Grillparzer's political views than he had previously permitted himself. Over the years, Grillparzer has been represented as a basically conservative figure, a representative of the old order with a strong emotional commitment to the Hapsburgs, to the imperial principle, and to the preservation of the unity of the empire.[1] Emphasis has been placed on his mistrust of democracy, his fear of revolution and of the masses, and on his defense of the humanitarian values of the eighteenth century.[2] His plays have also been felt to testify to his fundamentally conservative and monarchist principles, primarily because of his depiction of the two Rudolfs, the idealized emperor of *König Ottokar* and the emperor of *Ein Bruderzwist in Habsburg*, who is sympathetically portrayed as the desperate defender of the old feudal system. For W. E. Yates, his plays "attest his belief in an immutable order of things, whose political reflection is the hierarchical state."[3]

But Grillparzer's conservative image stems in the main from his conduct and attitude during the 1848 Revolution, and contrasts markedly with the reputation that he enjoyed prior to 1848 as a moderate liberal. Many of his earlier diary entries and political statements testify to his liberal views, even though in many cases they amount to little more than isolated reactions to events and experiences, and are not necessarily an expression of a consistently held political philosophy.[4] His numerous comments in his diaries on the repressive atmosphere of Metternich's Austria clearly derive from his own occasional brushes with the authorities. He saw Austria as a land hostile to poetry (IV, 400) and to the noblest spiritual aspirations (IV, 462). His life, in 1826, was an eternal conflict with stupidity and corruption (IV, 399). As early as 1810 he wished to flee the despotism and misery of Austria (IV, 257), and when ill in France in 1836 he could not even feel homesick, so disgraceful were the conditions in his own land (IV, 567). Many of his comments on the situation in Austria were prompted by his reactions to more favorable conditions experienced abroad. In 1826 he sensed a spirit of freedom in the liberal atmosphere of Berlin (IV, 423–4), in 1836 he was impressed with legal procedures in France (IV, 548–9), and with parliament in England (IV, 610–12). Some of his more radical statements were inspired by events abroad, such as the French July Revolution of 1830, when he asserted that it would be better for the people of France to progress toward a democratic form of government than to support the kind of constraints that he himself endured in Austria (IV, 461–2). In 1836 he could even find a logical argument with which to refute the opponents of the ideal of popular sovereignty (III, 1100).

Such remarks indicate a distinct desire for political reform, and suggest a degree of sympathy with the more radical trends of the time. However, by 1837 Grillparzer was more skeptical, stating that while democracy and republicanism may in theory be the two most desirable forms of government, they were in practice the two most dangerous ones (III, 1065). By 1838 he was expressing misgivings about the principle of popular sovereignty on the grounds that this simply meant that a government of a different type was given dictatorial powers (III, 1101), and in 1844 he implied that the people were in any case incapable of responsible government. While recognizing the necessity for a constitution in Prussia, and Austria too (III, 1073–4), he argued that the point of a constitution is not that the people should be permitted to govern themselves—they are rarely capable of this, he felt—but that the individual should enjoy some control over his own affairs (III, 1105). These are solid liberal views, in tune with moderate liberal opinion of his day, displaying a desire for political reform in an outmoded absolutist system, yet not going so far as to advocate democratic self-government for the people.

All his life Grillparzer seems to have fallen in line with liberal views of some form or other. In the earlier days of liberalism, when he himself was suffering under the oppressions of the Metternich regime, liberals were concerned primarily with securing for the individual a degree of personal freedom within the existing form of government.[5] At this time Grillparzer was impressed by the achievement of a more liberal atmosphere in Prussia and by the consequent popularity of the monarch. Later, in 1847, he stressed the need for a more liberal approach on the part of Europe's monarchs, advocating that they should show a greater interest in the welfare of their subjects. The implication is that not the form of government needs to be changed, but the attitude of individual rulers (III, 1039–40). Only in the 1830s, when Grillparzer himself seems to have gone through a more radical phase, did liberalism become politically more progressive. In the 1840s liberals tended to divide into the radicals, who stood for democracy, republicanism, and social reform, and the moderates, who advocated a constitution with a liberal monarch, equality before the law, and freedom of speech.[6] In view of his reservations concerning democracy and republicanism, it is clear that Grillparzer belonged to the more moderate camp. But it must also be stressed that both the moderates *and* the radicals at this time shared a profound distrust of the masses and feared popular revolution.[7] It was in this spirit that Grillparzer could refer in 1844 to his liberal views (IV, 689), yet also express his fears of communism, the full-scale socialist revolution to which the more radical trends might lead (III, 1008).

Between 1825, when he first frequented the Ludlamshöhle club, and the 1840s, when he was an active member of the Juridisch-politische Leseverein, Grillparzer associated with liberals such as Bauernfeld, Anton von Doblhoff, and Count Auersperg, and though he did not always sympathize with their most radical opinions (IV, 209–10), he signed the 1845 petition demanding relaxation of censorship. Grillparzer's moderate views are neither self-contradictory nor unique. His detestation of Austria's autocratic regime, his interest in radical political ideals, yet also his misgivings about the extremes to which such ideals might lead, are consistent with the attitude of many moderate liberals of his day. Nor did his liberalism prevent him from remaining an Austrian patriot. Much of his criticism of Metternich was based on his conviction that Metternich's policies were actually detrimental to Austria's political interests. He was clearly concerned that the unity of the empire should be preserved (III, 1019–21). The multinational character of the empire was in tune with his own supranational humanitarian ideals, and he felt that the nationalist movements, which were gaining ground among the individual subject peoples, represented a reversion to the barbarism of the dark ages. He thus retained a fundamental loyalty to the Hapsburg monarchy, a loyalty which had a decisive influence on his attitude toward the revolution of 1848.

It has generally been assumed that the events of 1848 marked a turning point in the development of Grillparzer's political views,[8] but in view of his moderate opinions it is difficult to see how he could have remained a whole-hearted supporter of the revolution. His reaction after the first three days (March 13–15) was favorable, for it seemed that the desired reforms, including abolition of censorship and the promise of a constitution, had been won with the minimum of disorder.[9] But from Grillparzer's viewpoint the situation rapidly deteriorated. Primarily, he objected to the behavior of the revolutionaries, as he saw the naive heroism of the early days degenerate into irresponsible and violent extremism. During April and May Vienna became more disorderly. Journals carried malicious attacks on respectable citizens, private property was threatened, and there were radical demands for popular sovereignty. The imperial family fled to Innsbruck, and on May 26 students went to the barricades, demanding that the government make radical electoral concessions. This has been regarded as the extreme left point of the revolution,[10] and it is hardly surprising that one already suspicious of the concept of popular sovereignty and fearful of a socialist revolution, should become disenchanted with what he perceived as a drift toward anarchy. In his address of May 1849 Grillparzer reminds Radetzky that the atrocities of 1848 were not caused by any initial failings on the part of the revolutionaries, but by the fact that the revolution eventually ran away with itself (III, 1050).

Grillparzer's second concern was that the revolution might bring about the disintegration of the empire, for it did indeed intensify, rather than reconcile, the nationalist interests, and this tendency prompted Grillparzer's famous poem "Feldmarschall Radetzky," published on June 8 in celebration of the victories of the imperial army over the Italian rebels. The poem reflects the awareness, which he shared with many Austrian patriots, of the paramount importance of the army for the survival of the empire as a whole, and his growing hostility toward the nationalism of the smaller ethnic groups. Grillparzer's third fear was that the conduct of the revolutionaries might eventually be self-defeating and might provoke a reaction from the more conservative sections of the population. These might regard the disorders as an inevitable consequence of freedom and might even prefer a regression to the pre-revolutionary situation, an ironic development which to the moderate liberal would be as unwelcome as the drift toward mob rule (III, 1044–8).

Grillparzer's withdrawal of support for the 1848 Revolution was inconsistent neither with his liberalism of the 1830s and 1840s nor with the attitude of the majority of moderate liberals of the time. The revolution was initially a bourgeois inspiration, so that when the orderly liberal revolt of March 13–15 threatened to turn into a disorderly revolution of the proletariat, many liberals deserted the cause and helped to foster the counterrevolution. Although it is easy to see why Grillparzer has been branded as a reactionary, his views of these events were not those of an inveterate conservative; rather they expressed the misgivings of one who was in principle in favor of political reform, but who became fearful of the consequences of the behavior of those involved. Nor do they point to the transformation of an "erstwhile liberal"[11] into a crusty reactionary. Grillparzer was already suspicious of left-wing trends, and the events of 1848 simply turned his doubts into real fears. Grillparzer did not wish matters to revert to the pre-revolutionary state, and he hoped in 1851 that Emperor Francis Joseph would not repeat the mistakes of the outmoded system (III, 1055). Indeed, he felt that the government of 1851 should be supported because it would put an end to the idiocies of the previous twenty or thirty years (IV, 720). When the government did, in fact, drift further to the right during the 1850s, Grillparzer became more disenchanted, being particularly dissatisfied with the Concordat with the Vatican of 1855.

Though they are not concerned exclusively with politics and certainly do not depict the kind of revolution that occurred in 1848, the three tragedies to be dealt with in this chapter do touch on the themes of political change and development, rebellion and reaction, and in particular on the concept of the state. Because of this they reflect Grillparzer's own ambivalent attitude toward the political events of his time, suggesting both his perception of a need for change and progress, and his fears of what might result from too radical a transformation of the prevailing political system.

II Libussa

In the composition of *Libussa* Grillparzer experienced as much difficulty as with any of his works. Its genesis goes back to the early 1820s, but progress was so intermittent that the tragedy was not completed until 1847. The main reason for the delay was Grillparzer's fear that, by the nature of the theme, he was being carried away from a treatment of human emotions into the realm of pure ideas and forced to write in a manner utterly foreign to his principles as a dramatist (IV, 387, 475). The plot of the tragedy is drawn from Czech mythology and is based on the legend of the foundation of the city of Prague in the ninth century by Přemysl, husband of the princess

Libuše and founder of the famous Přemislid dynasty. Grillparzer depicts the period as a major turning point in history, presenting the passing of a patriarchal and agrarian community and the dawn of the modern age of material progress and urban civilization. The tragedy thus has an obvious cultural and political theme, and although Grillparzer has introduced an emotional interest by presenting the cultural turning point symbolically in terms of the marriage of Libussa and Primislaus, it has, as Grillparzer feared, been interpreted primarily as a drama of ideas, namely, as an allegory of the transition of mankind from the golden age of natural innocence to a state of guilt and sin, from primitive barbarism and lawlessness to the civilized legal state. It has also been seen as exemplifying the conflict between contradictory historical and cultural concepts, between nature and technical progress, beauty and utilitarianism, the contemplative life and the active life, individualism and collectivism. [12]

The preoccupation of commentators with the tragedy's intellectual import has been matched by a critical neglect of its dramatic qualities, which is unfortunate, for the courtship of Libussa and Primislaus is presented with an appealing combination of innocent charm and subtle sophistication. Nevertheless, the very introduction of the love theme afforded Grillparzer further problems, for he had difficulty in linking it to the main cultural "idea." The result is an apparent lack of unity, suggested by obvious structural divisions, for each theme in turn is given emphasis in clearly defined stages. [13] Initially, the love theme is fleetingly struck when the princess Libussa encounters the peasant Primislaus while she is out in the forest. But after this brief prologue the first two acts are dominated by the political theme. When the death of Bohemia's patriarchal prince Krokus is reported, the crown is offered to each of his three daughters. The two older princesses refuse, but the youngest, Libussa, accepts, and Act II represents her attempt to found a model community. But her system of government is a failure, and recognizing the need for a strong ruler, she sends for Primislaus. Following this, the third and fourth acts are given over to the development of the relationship between lovers. Here again Libussa encounters difficulties, for Primislaus responds to her offer of marriage evasively and with pride. Only when Libussa humbles herself and begs, rather than commanding him to marry her, is a harmonious relationship achieved. Finally, in Act V, the political theme reasserts itself when Primislaus, as ruler now, asks Libussa to bless his new city and foretell its future. This she does, but only reluctantly, and her prophecy is full of pessimism. Exhausted by her efforts, she dies.

The looseness of the play's structure is accompanied by an uneven-
ness in mood and style. In the opening scene the atmosphere is
idyllic, and the early stages have a fairy-tale quality, appropriate to
the mythological material. Libussa's sisters have supernatural powers
and devote themselves to the contemplation of nature and the spirit;
their magical realm is separated from Primislaus's forest by the three
symbolic oak trees, the "Trennungs-Eichen"; and their speech occasionally has a mystical charm-like ring:

> Unter Sternen schweif ich,
> In der Tiefe walt ich;
> Was Natur vermag und kann,
> Ist mir willig untertan.   (207–10)

(Under the stars I rove, in the depths I rule. Whatever nature can do is
subject to my will.)

The minor characters are not drawn in detail, but as symbols or types,
possessing at most a single characteristic, such as "wise" Lapak,
"strong" Biwoy, and "mighty" Domaslav. There are riddles, coinci-
dences, and theatrical motifs reminiscent of the Viennese popular
stage. Particularly striking is the use of a visual symbol to reflect the
course of the relationship between Libussa and Primislaus.[14] This is
the golden chain that Libussa wears around her waist and that contains the jewel given to her by her father. When Primislaus removes
this jewel in the first scene, and places the chain around her neck, his
action suggests both the impression the encounter has made on her
heart and her consequent estrangement from her family. When in
Act II it is suggested to her that she should marry, she gives the now
incomplete chain to her three suitors, the three Wladiken, and sets
them a riddle about its missing part. From this it is clear that she can
only have Primislaus in mind as a possible husband, and when by
coincidence the Wladiken meet him and ask his help, he solves the
riddle and becomes aware of her feelings for him. But Primislaus
communicates with Libussa in kind, returning the jewel to her to
remind her of his existence, but keeping the chain. Only when the
two have reached a full psychological understanding is the jewel
returned to its original place and the chain becomes whole again.
During this fairy-tale sequence the action borders on comedy at the
expense of the bewildered Wladiken, and on farce when Libussa, in
anger at Primislaus's obstinacy, has him let down through a trap-door.

These elements appear to accord badly with the atmosphere of high
tragedy generated by the lofty style of the later speeches:

> Dan schließen sich des Himmels goldne Pforten,
> Begeisterung und Glauben und Vertraun,
> Und was herabträuft von den selgen Göttern,
> Nimmt nicht den Weg mehr zu der flachen Welt.   (2390–3)

(Then the golden gates of heaven will close, and inspiration, faith and trust,
and all else that falls like rain from the blessed gods, will no longer make its
way to the plains below.)

Once again Grillparzer has sought to achieve the apparently incongruous combination of the naive and the sophisticated, of the popular
and the refined.

In spite of the popular elements contained in the love sequence,
the relationship between Primislaus and Libussa is itself one of the
most sophisticated drawn by Grillparzer, for it eventually comes to
fruition not through any sudden realization of passion, but through a
shift in attitudes. Grillparzer is concerned with the intellectual aspects of the relationship rather than with an analysis of pure emotion.
In the early stages of the relationship there are only brief indications
of any emotional involvement, a pointed inquiry from Primislaus as to
whether any man may aspire to her hand, brief references by Libussa
to a secret of her heart and to a fleeting encounter with a man worthy
of her hand. But in the scene in which Primislaus encounters the
Wladiken he refers more explicitly to the passionate beating of his
heart, and his initial joy gives way to sorrow that she should have
entrusted everything to the chance solution of a riddle: "Farewell,
Good Fortune, your flight was much too swift!" For her part, Libussa
is reduced to despair when she hears that Primislaus has returned her
jewel in exchange for gold and she echoes Primislaus's own exclama-
tion: "Farewell, oh Hope, my first and now my last." These outbursts
are all the more touching for their brevity, and for the fact that there is
no open confession of feelings between the lovers, only indirect and
misinterpreted communications. But it is when Libussa sends for
Primislaus that the level of misunderstanding between them becomes critical. Feeling that Primislaus has spurned her, she decides
to impress him by commanding him to appear before her as her
subject. But this is a mistake, for Primislaus tells us that he would find

it degrading to be raised to a position of eminence simply through his wife's status. Moreover, he implies to Libussa that he cannot accept an offer of marriage merely as a reward for having given her hospitality, and would prefer to be appreciated for his own qualities as a man. Still Libussa fails to understand him, and tries to impress him further with the magnificence of her palace. Only when she hears him tell her servant Wlasta that a woman's strength lies in her weakness, in humility and mildness, does she herself become more humble. At this he is more willing to praise her as a sublime, heavenly creature, while she confesses her need for his strength and determination. The relationship is thus finally established on the basis of a mutual recognition of the other's value, on interdependence and humility, rather than on pride.

In view of the happy conclusion to Act IV and of the sympathetic treatment of the lovers during the love affair, the play's tragic outcome and the bleak pessimism of the major portion of Libussa's prophecy are something of a surprise. This is due partly to the fact that the political principles of Primislaus, which are primarily to blame, are not explicitly conveyed until he has taken power. Nevertheless, there are early indications of crucial differences in character and outlook between Libussa and Primislaus, which prepare us for the critical division which becomes evident in Act V. And although these differences initially affect the relationship only on a personal level, they do have political implications, so that the love theme and the political theme develop concurrently and not separately, as suggested by the structural divisions of the tragedy.

From the outset Libussa's political aspirations are closely associated with the new feelings aroused in her by Primislaus. Before the play begins she has shared in the life of her sisters, who hold themselves aloof from human affairs, but she now regards their preoccupation with abstract and remote phenomena as something monotonous and sterile. But though she experiences a warm glow of human emotion with the first stirrings of passion, she attempts first to realize her new attitude in the political, rather than the domestic sphere. Her model state is an egalitarian one, based on the altruistic ideals of brotherly love and mutual trust; individual rights and personal wealth are abolished and all work for the common good. Yet this earthly paradise is too idealistically conceived, for personal disputes occur and there are demands for individual rights and favors. Reluctantly Libussa perceives the need for a system of laws with which to maintain authority, but predicts that one day the people will look back to her brief rule with nostalgia:

> Wenn ihr dann klagt, trifft selber euch die Klage,
> Und ihr denkt etwa mein und an Libussens Tage.   (1004f.)

(When you lament, your lament will fall on yourselves, and you will think of me and of the days of Libussa's reign.)

Libussa's attempt to create a model society has foundered on the inability of the people to live up to her principles; yet these retain an intrinsic value, a beauty of their own, and remain in the memory as an unrealizable, conceptual ideal.

As well as being linked to her encounter with Primislaus, Libussa's ideals also appear to owe something to her identity as a woman; for her society has a matriarchal quality and her mild and gentle rule is contrasted with the patriarchal spirit in which her father reigned over the people. The Wladiken acknowledge her to be just, mild, wise and dignified, but would be happier if she had a man at her side. When Libussa recognizes the necessity for law and order, she decides that it must be the man Primislaus who should impose it, and when he appears she draws an explicit distinction between her own wisdom and piety and his cleverness (*Klugheit*). Here Grillparzer has depicted the woman as the creature of principle and endowed her with an intuitive wisdom and goodness, mildness and gentleness, humanitarian virtues of civilization which Goethe also embodied in a female character, Iphigenie; to the man Grillparzer has given the practical ability and tenacity (*Beharrlichkeit*) to enforce the law. In a sense, therefore, the political problem has been presented symbolically in terms of the differences between the sexes, and Libussa has indeed been viewed as an early example of a "modern" woman who has attempted to bring both her ideals and femininity into political life, where the masculine qualities of toughness and strength are most needed.[15]

The awakening of love in Libussa's heart has directed her first into an alien sphere where the attributes of her sex are unfortunately unsuited to the demands of reality. Her values are appropriate to the marital or family situation, not to the business of government.[16] For Primislaus there is a more fundamental problem, for he feels that her position as ruler is incompatible with her identity as a woman. A woman may be worshipped as a thing of beauty and for her essential nobility, but her value is intrinsic, and a man must still protect her because of her weakness. Though, in marriage, she may retain her status as a sublime being, the husband must yet be master in his own house. We have, then, a potentially ironic situation in which Libussa's femininity ensures her political failure, while her political position threatens to prevent her fulfillment as a human being. Even though this problem is solved, at least from Primislaus's viewpoint, when Libussa subordinates herself to him as wife and subject, the major moral problem remains. For although Libussa reverts in a technical sense to her feminine role, as wife and mother, she retains in her heart the political principles that she displayed as ruler.

When Libussa sends for Primislaus, she does so not simply because he possesses qualities that she lacks, but because she feels that only he is capable of pursuing a political course that is alien to her nature and principles. Thus it is hardly surprising that when Primislaus takes command his principles are not hers. Basically their aims are similar, to foster a community in which all work for the common good, but whereas Libussa's reign was benign and was based on an assumption of the essential goodness of man, Primislaus enforces his policy with an iron hand and measures everything according to its practical usefulness. For Libussa, her little community had a value of its own, but Primislaus envisages the ceaseless intellectual and practical progress of mankind. Libussa's community retained its primitive ties with nature, and though she abolished traditional rights and privileges and placed the value of the community above that of the individual, she demonstrates that she believes in the sanctity and integrity of each individual human being. Primislaus, however, builds a city which, from Libussa's point of view, is severing the bond between man and nature; in doing so, he is contemptuously disregarding the interests of particular individuals by tearing down the forests, and is creating an institution in which people will be crowded together and so lose their individuality. Libussa thus finds herself at odds with her husband politically, and her concluding prophecy represents an extension of her misgivings concerning Primislaus's methods and principles, as she predicts how they may be realized in terms of social and political developments. She envisages a materialistic society, dominated by greed. Men will still have ideals, but these will lead only to hatred and war, generated by religious or ideological strife, while concepts such as freedom and equality will be abused to further the selfish interests of particular groups.

Libussa begins her prophecy by describing Primislaus's venture in terms of the Fall of Man, an analogy which, by extension, suggests that her own rule may be viewed as a brief golden age of innocence, a kind of earthly paradise, incorporating values that human beings were tragically unable to support. By contrast, Primislaus's society is soulless and empty of spiritual values. Because of this distinction it is misleading to interpret the tragedy solely in terms of a contrast between the "active" life undertaken by Libussa at the outset, and the "contemplative" life pursued by her sisters, and of which she herself was originally a devotee.[17] Admittedly, such an interpretation is encouraged by the clear division made between these two opposing spheres. Her sisters insist that once she has ventured into the realm of human affairs she may not return to her former existence, and they even attribute her death to contamination arising from contact with people. Their attitude has suggested to some critics that Libussa's tragic guilt, like that of Sappho, resides in her desire to transcend the limitations of her character and original surroundings, to forsake a higher destiny for a life of activity, which she could not endure.[18] It is certainly true that she cannot return to her former life, but as the sisters realize, this is because she is in love (1158f.). Nor does she necessarily wish to, for her prophecy is undertaken only to please Primislaus. The sisters themselves are presented throughout as unsympathetic creatures, and Libussa's renunciation of her life with them is seen as a positive rather than a negative or tragic move. She leaves her ivory tower for fundamentally unselfish reasons, for the sake of the happiness of others. In her prophecy she is concerned entirely with the nature of actual political developments, and what she laments is not her own renunciation of the contemplative life, but the passing of her ideal social and political values, the love of one's neighbor, reverence for the individual, trust. It is in their passing, symbolized finally by Libussa's death, that the tragedy of the play resides.

Because of Libussa's love of humanity, which so distinguishes her from her sisters, her prophecy takes an unexpected turn toward the conclusion of the play. Her recognition that man is essentially good (*Der Mensch ist gut*) encourages her to conclude that after the period of material progress man will come to acknowledge his spiritual emptiness, and love, inspiration, and a spirit of humility—significantly the quality which cemented the union between Primislaus and Libussa—will once again return to society. Libussa envisages a long period during which mankind must develop and progress, learning essentially by experience until ready to adopt the values that she herself found to be hitherto impracticable. For some critics, the tenor of Libussa's final assertions lends the tragedy an Hegelian quality,[19] but it is not a synthesis of opposing values or principles that Libussa predicts. She looks forward not to progress itself, but to an eventual reversal to former values after a period of error. Her attitude is an ambivalent one, deploring the developments of the future, yet recognizing the educative purposes that these might serve.

Clearly it is arguable that Libussa's prophecy also reflects the ambivalence of Grillparzer's own attitude toward the political events of his time and of his own assessment of the future, particularly as we are given to understand that the prophecy is divinely inspired and presumably intended to represent a vision of truth. Moreover, although it is couched only in vague terms, there are occasional references to such specific phenomena as the political rise of Germany and the nineteenth-century middle-class values of efficiency and honesty. In these Heinz Politzer has detected traces of Grillparzer's detestation of German nationalism,[20] and in Libussa's attitude to Primislaus's principles W. E. Yates has perceived Grillparzer's own critique of the self-interested materialism of his society, as "evils masquerading under the slogans of liberty and equality":

> Das Edle schwindet von der weiten Erde,
> Das Hohe sieht vom Niedern sich verdrängt.
> Und Freiheit wird sich nennen die Gemeinheit,
> Als Gleichheit brüsten sich der dunkle Neid. (2384–7)

(Nobility will disappear from the world, the sublime will be supplanted by the vulgar. And baseness will act in the name of freedom, and dark envy will pose as equality.)[21]

Certainly this sheds further light on Grillparzer's reservations regarding the forces that were pushing Germany toward revolution. But in Libussa's attitude toward Primislaus's legal system, which subjugates the interests of the individual to the requirements of the whole, we may also see reflected Grillparzer's own hostility toward the repressive police state of Metternich. Libussa is lamenting the passing of humanitarian ideals which Grillparzer not only fears will have no part in the materialistic society to come, but which he also already finds absent in his own. Likewise, Libussa's recognition that man is not yet ready to support the values that she attempted to introduce, recalls Grillparzer's view that people are not capable of democratic self-government (III, 1105), to be borne out by the disorderly behavior of the revolutionaries which he found so abhorrent.

The play itself does not present a revolution as such, yet its theme is political and social change. Of considerable significance, then, is the surprisingly optimistic conclusion to Libussa's prophecy, her assertion of the goodness of her man, her vision of a new golden age, her faith in the return of humanitarian values.

This conclusion forms too substantial a part of the whole prophecy—about one quarter—to be ignored, and so to a considerable extent outweighs the pessimism of her earlier statements.[22] Particularly interesting is her prediction that however odious future developments may be in themselves, they may yet have a beneficial long-term effect. Libussa is finally able to take a more positive view of Primislaus's activities than she has conveyed hitherto. Previously she has recognized the necessity for his presence at the head of her community, has even acknowledged that he is right in almost all matters (1961), and though out of sympathy with his new undertaking, is determined to give it her blessing (2276). Now she sees that because of his innate goodness, man's development along the undesirable lines proposed by Primislaus may yet serve to bring about a desirable result. This is only a guarded affirmation of progress, and the improvement that she envisages is vaguely conceived and remote in time. If her words are indicative of any hopeful feelings in Grillparzer himself, he is clearly looking forward to a period well beyond that of the foreseeable future. Yet they do provide undeniable evidence of his own ultimate faith in humanity, suggested previously in his sympathetic treatment of human emotions in *Des Meeres und der Liebe Wellen* and *Weh dem, der lügt!* and of the conviction which he obviously holds at this time that humanitarian values will eventually triumph over barbarism.

III   Ein Bruderzwist in Habsburg

Grillparzer was preoccupied for many years with his final historical tragedy, *Ein Bruderzwist in Habsburg* [Fraternal Strife in Hapsburg]. His studies on the material go back to his earliest days, and the play was planned in detail and actually begun in the 1820s. But before he had completed the first act, work came to an abrupt halt in 1828 and he did not resume it until the 1840s, eventually completing the first version just before the outbreak of the revolution in 1848. *Ein Bruderzwist* deals with the period that led directly into the chaos of the Thirty Years' War and is Grillparzer's most profoundly pessimistic work. Because the age which he portrays has so many features in common with his own, this tragedy has come to be regarded as his fullest exposition of contemporary political developments, his political testament, expressing not only his own fears of the coming revolution, but also offering to posterity a nightmare vision of the twentieth century. Hugo von Hofmannsthal praised it as the most significant historical and political tragedy written in the German language, and as a dramatic interpretation of an historical epoch it has been compared with Hofmannsthal's own late tragedy, *Der Turm* [The Tower].[23]

Grillparzer's *Bruderzwist* spans the years 1594 to 1618, one of the most complex periods in Hapsburg history. But as was the case with *König Ottokar* he again condenses and simplifies the historical material. Here he concentrates on the situation facing the emperor Rudolph II (1576–1612), who as guardian of the interests of the Catholic Church had to contend with the situation following the Reformation, when so many of the subjects of the empire had adopted the Protestant faith. The main action of the tragedy is initiated by Rudolf's decision to entrust his ambitious and incompetent brother Mathias with the command of the imperial army, which is engaged in defending the frontiers of the empire against the Turks in Hungary. Act II presents the resulting inefficiency and disorganization in the conduct of the war, and the ensuing conference which is masterminded by Mathias's unscrupulous adviser, Archbishop Klesel. Through his cunning methods Klesel manipulates the Hapsburg archdukes into making peace with the Turks in Rudolf's absence and against his will, and subsequently into granting Mathias full powers to act in the emperor's name. In Act III, the pivot of the drama, attention reverts to Rudolf, who learns that by promising concessions to the Protestants in Hungary and Austria, Mathias has risen in popularity. The danger to Rudolf's authority increases when Mathias invades Bohemia, where Rudolf has his court in Prague. At this point the Bohemian Protestants exploit the situation by forcing Rudolf to sign the *Majestätsbrief,* a charter that will legitimize their religion. This ensures Rudolf of their military support, but, not wishing to initiate a civil war, Rudolf allows Mathias to enter Prague unopposed. Nevertheless, when his nephew Archduke Leopold offers to restore Rudolf's authority by attacking Prague with an army he holds in Passau, Rudolf allows himself momentarily to be carried away by a desire for vengeance on Mathias, and agrees. But Leopold's invasion in Act IV serves only to cement an alliance between Mathias and the Bohemians, and Leopold's defeat undermines Rudolf's political posi-

tion altogether. In Act V the scene shifts to Vienna where Mathias and
Klesel have assumed the reins of power. But their attempts to enforce
the legalization of Protestantism in Bohemia have brought them into
conflict with the fanatical Catholic, Archduke Ferdinand, who succeeds in removing Klesel, so rendering Mathias himself politically
impotent. In reaction to a Protestant uprising in Prague, Ferdinand
and his general Wallenstein begin planning a punitive expedition
against the rebels, so embarking on the first military campaign of the
Thirty Years' War.

Although interest shifts during the play between the three main
Hapsburg figures, critical attention has been focussed primarily on
the emperor Rudolf, one of Grillparzer's most problematic and fascinating creations, who in his own way makes as dramatic an impression as any of Grillparzer's characters. When Rudolf first appears
before his assembled court, Grillparzer gives us a brief but vivid
portrait of the legendary, half-mad recluse. He scarcely speaks,
producing only short, impatient exclamations, shows greater interest
in works of art and literature than in political dispatches, repeatedly
demands to be left alone, and when confronted with reports of the
war in Hungary, refuses to listen and angrily bangs on the floor with
his stick. Beneath this eccentric exterior there is a second Rudolf, the
visionary philosopher who emerges in his private conversations with
Archduke Ferdinand in Act I, and his friend Duke Julius in Act III. To
Ferdinand he explains that his political inactivity derives from his
astrological studies, from his perception that the stars still exist in
harmony with God's laws, in contrast with the world of human affairs,
where selfishness and confusion abound. Rudolf prefers to con-
template the order of the heavenly bodies with reverence, rather
than interfere in the uncertain world of politics. Yet in Act III we see
that Rudolf's preoccupations are not exclusively celestial, for he has
translated his observations into a political policy, based on his conception of the state as an earthly reflection of the heavenly order,
which it is his duty as ruler to uphold. This order is at present
threatened by the growth of Protestantism, carrying with it the awful
prospect of a civil war, which may arise from any clash between the
Catholic and Protestant factions. Consequently, Rudolf's aim is to
maintain peace within the confines of the empire by holding the
hostile forces in a state of balance. Caught between Protestant claims
for the recognition of their religion and Catholic demands for its
suppression, he has attempted to avoid outright conflict by not leaning too much to one side, by steering a middle course of toleration and

refusing either to sanction the persecution of Protestants or to grant them official recognition (1567f.). It is also in the cause of internal peace that he has allowed the war in Hungary to go on, hoping thereby to keep Catholic and Protestant united against the common enemy (1186–92). His policy, which is in effect one of nonintervention, also reflects his ethical views, for in refusing to commit himself to the support of one particular group, he remains free from the selfishness that he condemns in others. His refusal to recognize Protestantism officially also accords with his view of the new faith as a threat to the political system of his day, and his fears in this respect are conveyed when he tells the Bohemians that the concessions made according to the terms of the *Majestätsbrief* would produce an avalanche of demands right through the social and political hierarchy, with ensuing lawlessness, anarchy, and mob rule.

Rudolf's vision of an eternal order in the stars has been represented as a positive faith in an ideal source of values beyond the reach of ordinary mortals,[24] while his insight into the political situation has encouraged the assumption that he possesses a depth of wisdom and moral integrity far superior to those of his fellowmen, that he is essentially the innocent victim of the imperfections of others.[25] Consequently, it has been assumed that like Libussa he is to be regarded as Grillparzer's own mouthpiece, expressing the author's reverence for the divine order of creation, his respect for the Hapsburg imperial tradition and for the institution of the state, and suggesting the more conservative position toward which Grillparzer was allegedly moving in the 1840s. With Libussa, Rudolf shares the vision of the ideological war to come, a major conflagration which will be sparked off by forces existing within society itself, religious strife, materialistic greed, and the clamor for political rights:

> Bis endlich aus der untersten der Tiefen
> Ein Scheusal aufsteigt, gräßlich anzusehn,
> Mit breiten Schultern, weitgespaltnem Mund,
> Nach allem lüstern und durch nichts zu füllen.   (1247–50)

(Until finally from the lowest of the depths a monster will arise, hideous to look at, with broad shoulders and gaping jaws, greedy for everything and satisfied by nothing.)

Rudolf's speeches certainly seem to convey Grillparzer's fears of what revolution might entail and his distrust of the masses, and it is easy to appreciate why Rudolf's vision of destruction and upheaval should have been seen to anticipate correctly some of the events of our own times.

Yet, although Rudolf's speeches may be viewed favorably within the context of subsequent historical developments, they have to be judged in conjunction with the political situation as presented in the play itself. Unlike Libussa, Rudolf is not simply a prophet, an onlooker, but a man with political responsibilities of whom action is required. In their assessment of Rudolf most commentators have pointed to the contrast between the purity of his vision and the fallibility of his actions, to the tragic paradox of the play that the best man is also a weak man.[26] As he sits pondering the heavens, he admits that he is weak and incompetent, incapable of governing, and we have glimpses of a doddering old man, physically frail and lapsing into meaningless incoherence (as in 434–9). Yet it is also clear that the very nature of Rudolf's vision and the lesson he draws from it must themselves bear some responsibility for the political confusion. His translation of the divine order of the stars into the worldly institution of the state is arguably little more than a justification of the political status quo, a rationalization of his reverence for the religious, political, and social institutions of his day, namely the Catholic Church, the Holy Roman Empire, and the feudal hierarchy.[27] All of these he regards as permanent institutions on which civilization has been based, which exist in their own right and which he fears may be destroyed by any social or political change. His policy of avoiding civil strife is intrinsically noble, but his passivity comes over as a rigid refusal to make any concessions to the forces of progress. And if Rudolf's deliberations have told him that in the field of politics he can do nothing, his effective withdrawal from political affairs is just as diastrous as the activities of others, for as Julius reminds him, while he studies in his tower the disruptive forces in his empire are on the march:

> Ihr seid verraten, hoher Herr, verkauft.
> Indes ihr lernt, lehrt ihr der Welt den Aufruhr,
> Der schon entfesselt tobt in euern Städten.   (1330–2)

(My Lord, you are betrayed, deceived. While you are studying you are nurturing turmoil in the world, which is already raging freely in your cities.)

Most critically, Rudolf's failure to keep himself informed of the details of events means that he is unaware that Klesel is at Mathias's elbow and that the danger to his authority is real. It is precisely at this point in Act III, when he is faced with a crisis of his own making that requires decisive action, that his limitations are most obviously exposed. When the Bohemians demand his signature on the *Majestätsbrief*, he is caught in a dilemma, for if he refuses to conciliate their demands he will almost certainly yield his custodianship of peace and balance in the empire to the advancing Mathias; if, on the other hand, he signs, he will, in his own opinion, risk a social revolution. Either way, therefore, he must compromise on an aspect of his policy, but his response to the situation seems contradictory, irrational even, for by signing the charter and then forbidding the Bohemians to oppose Mathias, he both sacrifices his policy and the military advantage which he has thereby gained. Obviously, the situation is so complex that it is impossible for him to see his way clearly through it, but the fact remains that as a result of his irresolution he finds himself in a worse position than before. Then follows the coup de grace with his acceptance of Leopold's offer of military assistance from Passau, an action whereby Rudolf fleetingly but willfully forsakes his principles altogether and behaves in a selfish and aggressive manner, so touching off, for the most ignoble reasons, the civil war which he has striven so hard to avoid. Thus Rudolf himself makes the final contribution to his own downfall and humiliation, and the chaos and confusion of the fighting which is briefly glimpsed in the opening scene of Act IV provides a foretaste of the destruction of the Thirty Years' War.

Rudolf's actions in Act III have the effect of casting him in a less impressive or heroic light than would seem appropriate from the wisdom of his reflective speeches. He correctly forecasts the future holocaust, but neither his policies nor eventually his own nature can prevent it from coming about. Rudolf is another of Grillparzer's problematic characters, admirable in some respects, a failure in others. He fades from the play in a pathetic, unheroic fashion, humiliated and politically impotent, a prisoner in his own castle. Yet he retains a quiet dignity, facing his new situation with resignation and eventual pleasure that he has shed the burdens of office. In Rudolf, as in Bancbanus, Grillparzer has created a particularly sympathetic anti-hero, humane, well-intentioned and pious, yet also fallible and limited.

We have seen that Rudolf's policy of nonintervention is based primarily on his fear that the recognition of Protestantism will have serious political repercussions. Yet, although we do hear rumblings of political rebellion associated with the Protestant demands, the Protestants who appear are not presented unsympathetically. One of these is Duke Julius, Rudolf's most loyal friend, while the Bohemian nobles approach Rudolf with courtesy and regard his signature on their charter as a guarantee of stability and of their own rights and privileges, rather than the opposite (1514–31). The most obvious danger to stability comes from Rudolf's immediate entourage, members of his own family, who embody the characteristics of the age that he most condemns, vanity, selfishness, and willfulness. Mathias is Grillparzer's final portrait of the ambitious type, a mixture of vanity and weakness, eventually to be condemned by Rudolf for his empty heroics. In that he cannot rise to power by his own efforts, needing the assistance of Klesel, he recalls Ottokar and Rustan; but what is new about this character is his lack of exaltation once he has attained power. He is at first puzzled and confused, then desires only to be left in peace from the political troubles, and would prefer, ironically, to exchange places with the dead brother he deposed. Finally, he concludes the tragedy with a brief, but eloquent admission of his own guilt, a dramatic advertisement of the futility of ambition: "Mea culpa, mea culpa, mea maxima culpa."

But it is Archbishop Klesel who is arguably the villain of the tragedy, equally ambitious, but courageous and decisive. It is he who encourages Mathias to beg for the command of the army in Hungary, and who, during the conference in Act II, engineers the elevation of Mathias to full power. In this scene the methods of this cunning politician are seen to their best effect, for, although he says little, he succeeds in his objectives in the face of the blatant hostility of the archdukes Max, Ferdinand, and Leopold. Klesel is an unscrupulous, self-seeking opportunist, and we understand that it is he, a Catholic, who is later instrumental in furthering Mathias's political elevation by promising concessions to the Hungarian Protestants. The danger to stability lies not in Protestantism as such, but in the exploitation of the religious issue for personal gain, a phenomenon which was to bedevil the course of the Thirty Years' War to come, and which in an ideological context was to become, as Grillparzer feared, a feature of the 1848 Revolution. Yet once in possession of power, Klesel seems to change roles, pursuing in Act V what appears to be an enlightened and responsible policy toward the Protestants, encouraging them to build their churches in accordance with the terms of their charter and in the interests of peace. Klesel claims to be moving with the times, and now that he is acting in the interests of the whole rather than of his own advancement, his policy compares favorably even with Rudolf's former policy of neutrality and nonintervention. Yet eventually Klesel's policy of appeasement provokes the hostility of Ferdinand who interferes with Klesel's activities in Bohemia, so inciting the Protestant rebellion, the Defenestration of Prague of 1618. Ferdinand is the religious fanatic of the play, the representative of the Catholic reaction, whose cruelty toward the Protestants of his own duchy we have already seen horrify the more humane Rudolf (498–500). Now in the heady atmosphere of the preparations for war he sends Wallenstein to suppress the Bohemian rebels, and himself embarks with undisguised enthusiasm and confidence on a program of persecution in the Hapsburg territories. In one respect, therefore, Rudolf has been proved right, for in leaning too heavily toward the Protestant side Klesel has again rocked the boat and initiated the kind of clash between Catholic and Protestant that Rudolf tried to avoid. Ultimately, both Rudolf and Klesel have failed to avert the conflict; yet, significantly, it is the forces of reaction that initiate the holocaust, and their belligerent followers look forward with glee to a war which, as Grillparzer reminds us in their confident forecasts, will last for thirty years. If Grillparzer is here drawing an analogy with events of his own day, then we may recall that his hostility toward the revolution arose partly from his fears that the disorderly conduct of the revolutionaries might provoke a serious reaction from conservative forces.

Despite the nature of its theme, which suggests a political conflict on the grand scale, *Ein Bruderzwist* has never been regarded as one of Grillparzer's more theatrical plays. Considerable attention is focused on the primarily passive figure of Rudolf, and apart from brief sequences in Acts II and IV, Grillparzer avoids spectacular scenes of action, concentrating instead on intimate discussions, often between only two characters at a time, while the momentous events of history proceed offstage. Furthermore, although various characters, particularly Rudolf, are active in the sense that they take decisions that have important dramatic consequences, Grillparzer does not over-dramatize their decisions and activities, apparently deliberately refusing to capitalize on their dramatic potential. For example, Rudolf's decision to appoint Mathias to the command of the army is taken reluctantly and rapidly, with little argument or consideration of consequences, and is communicated almost in passing to Ferdinand, rather than to Mathias himself. Similarly, his decision to sign the Bohemians' charter is taken impulsively and unexpectedly after a long period of delay, while his authorization of Leopold's fatal attack on Prague even occurs offstage. The discreet handling of this major blemish on Rudolf's career is in keeping with the treatment of the

whole sequence of episodes in Act II relating to the recruitment of the
Passau army. The topic is alluded to in an atmosphere of
conspiracy—there are surreptitious references, vague suggestions,
short furtive discussions—so that it seems appropriate that Rudolf
should take his decision behind closed doors. All of these decisions
are taken in contradiction of his better judgment or principles, so that
in playing down the drama of these incidents it seems that Grillparzer
is deliberately minimizing the dramatic impact of his hero's guilt. But
there may be another reason for his refusal to exploit to the full the
dramatic potential of these moments, which is more directly related
to the general thematic material of the play. Because Rudolf appears
at these moments to be acting against his will—this is particularly the
case in the incident involving Leopold, for Rudolf runs from the stage
deliberately, to avoid exposing himself to temptation—we sense a
lack of control over the situation on his part. His decisions are taken
hastily, when he is under pressure; they are not the results of deliberate planning. A similar effect is obtained when the archdukes agree to
make peace with the Turks and to grant Mathias full powers. Ferdinand stares at the document, clearly "disagreeing" with the decision to which he has just been a signatory:

FERDINAND   *unterzeichnend.*
            Und hier die Unterschrift.

MAX   *ebenso.*   Sowie die meine.

FERDINAND   *der aufgestanden ist.*
            Wenn ich betrachte dieses Unglücksblatt,
            So gehts durch meine Seele wie Verderben.   (1046–8)

(F *signing*: Here is my signature. M *likewise:* And mine too. F *having risen:*
As I look at this unhappy document, I feel it in my soul that it will lead to
ruin.)

The impression conveyed is that events are assuming an independent
momentum of their own, beyond the control of the characters who
are initiating them.

The sense of helplessness generated at such moments accords with
the impression given by Grillparzer that the characters are faced with
a problem to which there is no obvious solution. Neither Rudolf's
policy of laissez-faire nor the firm actions undertaken at various times
by characters such as Klesel, Leopold, or Ferdinand represent the
right course, for all contribute directly or indirectly to the outbreak of

a war which becomes more inevitable as the tragedy progresses. The action of *Ein Bruderzwist* represents what amounts to a revolutionary situation in which dissenting groups are demanding rights and freedoms, a situation threatening, from Rudolf's viewpoint, social and political upheaval, the rule of the masses, civil war, and the disintegration of the empire. In this situation Grillparzer demonstrates that the danger to peace comes as much from those who exploit the grievances of the rebels as from the rebels themselves, that the threat from the forces of reaction is equally, if not more acute, that the persistent refusal to make concessions on the part of Rudolf in *Ein Bruderzwist,* as of Chancellor Metternich in Grillparzer's Austria, may be just as disastrous as a policy of appeasement.

Grillparzer's tendency in this tragedy to play down the drama of moments of decision, and to suggest that the characters are losing control of events, has for some critics highlighted a fundamental distinction between the atmosphere created here and that evoked in Schiller's historical tragedies. In *Ein Bruderzwist* there is an apparent absence of freedom of choice, none of the careful planning and tortuous deliberations which Schiller presented on the part of his Wallenstein and Queen Elizabeth. This has led Claude David to suggest that in presenting his characters as being essentially dependent on outside circumstances, pushed about like figures on the chessboard, Grillparzer is more of a Realist than Schiller.[28] Further, Edward McInnes argues that Grillparzer departs in *Ein Bruderzwist* from the Schillerian conception of history as a product of the human will, and comes close to the historical fatalism embodied in Büchner's *Dantons Tod* [Danton's Death].[29] It is true that the tragic outcome of *Ein Bruderzwist* is hardly presented as the product of the grand design of some inspired or powerful individual; and the atmosphere of inevitability does lend this tragedy a fatalistic flavor. Nonetheless, we should not lose sight of the fact that it is the characters themselves who initiate the events and who must ultimately bear the responsibility for the catastrophic outcome. Admittedly, many of the characters are not fully developed, but they come across as types rather than as rounded individuals. This is because Grillparzer concentrates on those qualities in his characters that bear directly on the political situation, on the ambition and vacillation of Mathias, the cunning opportunism of Klesel, the religious fanaticism of Ferdinand, and the uncontrolled enthusiasm of Leopold. These are the qualities that, in combination, serve to hasten the catastrophe into which the characters unintentionally blunder. If events seem at times to be moving

independently of human control, this is because of the proliferation in
this tragedy of human feelings, to which *Ein Bruderzwist* is
Grillparzer's most comprehensively pessimistic monument.

Despite the emphasis placed on the political rather than the private sphere, not all the characters are portrayed within such a limited
context. One character with a private life not even loosely connected
with the main political plot is Rudolf's natural son Don Cäsar. The
"story" surrounding this character is not drawn in any detail, and
aspects of it are left deliberately obscure, as Grillparzer's primary
interest is in the presentation of Cäsar's moods and manner in brief,
isolated episodes. We see him vainly challenging the forces of the law
to plead for the life of his friend Russworm, who has been condemned
for murder; pursuing Lukrezia, the girl he apparently loves, on a
journey through Hungary; breaking out of prison to join in the
confusion of the fighting resulting from Leopold's attack on Prague;
confronting Lukrezia with an accusation of infidelity and shooting her
when she denies this. Much has been written on the function of this
extraordinary character, whose characteristics are grotesquely exaggerated in the remarkably Expressionistic episodes in which he appears. Many critics, following Rudolf's own condemnation of him as
the true child of his turbulent age, see in him a dramatic embodiment
of the evils that Rudolf most abhors—a disrespect for the authority of
the law, a susceptibility to selfish and violent passions.

It is in the sense of a symbolic gesture against the imperfection of
the age that we may understand Rudolf's final harsh judgment upon
him. After he has been imprisoned again, we hear that Cäsar rages so
wildly that blood is let from his arm to quiet him. Subsequently he
tears off the bandages, but Rudolf, in dropping the key to his prison
down a well, refuses doctors access to him, so ensuring that he will
bleed to death. The prospect of Cäsar's intemperate passions ebbing
away with his life blood provides a striking anticipation of the destruction of the age which will be bled white by the coming war. At the
same time, Rudolf's judgment on Cäsar, though cruel, is not pro-
nounced without emotion, for Rudolf weeps as he condemns him,
and we are reminded that it is his own flesh and blood that he is
deliberately allowing to destroy itself. G. A. Wells has argued that
Rudolf's effective murder of his son is simply a demonstration of his
ability to punish the immorality and selfishness of the individual, in
contrast to his failure to subdue the various political forces which
confront him.[30] Yet this interpretation of the figure's function ignores
not only the association in Rudolf's mind of Cäsar with the forces of

the age itself, but also the personal relationship existing between Cäsar and himself. The ties of blood cannot be overlooked in an interpretation of Cäsar's role, and there is some evidence, as Heinz Politzer[31] and Eve Mason[32] have suggested, that Rudolf recoils from his son as from his own alter ego. Although Rudolf could not be compared even remotely with this wild and uncontrollable creature, he does eventually succumb to selfish emotions of his own when he authorizes Leopold's attack. It is not so very far-fetched to suggest that Grillparzer's presentation of Rudolf's own son is a symbolic reminder that Rudolf, the chief critic of the age, is also a major contributor to its chaos and destruction.

IV Die Jüdin von Toledo

In order to complete *Libussa* and *Ein Bruderzwist*, Grillparzer had put aside his recent work on a play of a very different character whose subject matter reflected preoccupations of his early and middle years. Grillparzer returned to this tragedy after the 1848 Revolution, completing it in the 1850s, and it was given its title, *Die Jüdin von Toledo* [The Jewess of Toledo], when it was first performed in Prague in 1872.

Ostensibly *Die Jüdin* is a historical tragedy set in medieval Spain. But there are few details of historical background, its plot is a simple one, and after the heavy political speeches of *Libussa* and *Ein Bruderzwist*, it initially makes a more lightweight impression. In its early stages it reflects Grillparzer's former predilection for the psychological study of passion, for the main interest is the legendary relationship betwen King Alfonso VIII of Castile and a Jewess. Nevertheless, the tragedy does have a political theme, which becomes more prominent in the later stages and which is indicative of Grillparzer's own shift in interest when he resumed work on the play. The first three acts are devoted to the love affair that begins when a young Jewish girl, Rahel, seeks safety from a hostile crowd in the royal garden of Toledo. She encounters King Alfons, who offers her protection in a garden-house nearby. There he visits her, is fascinated by her charms, and subsequently takes her to the castle of Retiro as his mistress. Meanwhile, the country is in danger of an invasion by the Moors, and in Act IV the nobles, alarmed at the king's neglect of the situation, assemble to take matters into their own hands. Their priority is that Alfons should return to his duty, something which may only be achieved by the removal of Rahel. The queen presses for her death, and eventually they proceed to Retiro to murder her. Alfons is bitterly angered, but is also made to admit his own guilt in the affair, and determines to atone by leading his army in the coming battle.

Grillparzer's combination in *Die Jüdin* of a love interest with a political theme is reminiscent of his treatment of such material in *Ein treuer Diener*, for once again he is concerned with a situation in which the very nature of the office of monarch seems to demand a devotion to duty at the expense of private feelings and personal development. The central character in *Die Jüdin* is the king himself, and in the first act, in which the psychological background to Alfons's case is sketched in, Grillparzer shows that the love affair springs directly from the nature of the king's political position. Having been made king as a child, Alfons has been concerned entirely with his political duties and has spent most of his time with his army. In this way he has remained perfect (*fleckenlos*), but, as he realizes himself, only because he has had no contact with what he calls the "good things of life."[33] He lacks real human experience and, most significantly, knew nothing of women before his marriage. In pursuit of his duties as monarch he has sacrificed his full development as a human being, and has remained cut off from the pleasures and pains of ordinary life. Even his marriage has made little difference, for he also finds his queen too "perfect." She is cold, ungrateful, and on her own admission finds sexual relations repulsive (1204). Alfons cannot love her warmly, is exasperated by her prudery, and thus dangerously susceptible to Rahel's charms. At first Rahel is depicted as a harmless little girl, and her approach to the king seems nothing more than the expression of a naive desire to be admired as a pretty child:

> Ich muß mal den König sehen
> Und er mich, ja, ja, er mich.
> Wenn er kommt und wenn er fragt:
> Wer ist dort die schöne Jüdin?
> Sag, wie heißt du?—Rahel, Herr!
> Isaaks Rahel! sprech ich dann.
> Und er kneipt mich in die Backen.
> Heiße dann die schöne Rahel.   (69–76)

(I must see the king just once, and he me, yes he me. When he comes and asks: Who is that beautiful Jewess? I say, what's your name? I shall say: Rahel, sir! Isaak's Rahel! And he will pinch my cheeks. Then I shall be called beautiful Rahel.)

The innocent charm of these short lines with their swift and insistent trochaic rhythm contrasts with the more measured tones of the king and his courtiers, with their effusive speeches delivered in the longer iambic pentameters. The king, too, regards Rahel as a child, a source of harmless amusement. Apparently she is full of fun and laughter at home, and this is borne out when we see her play-acting in the garden-house, dressing up in carnival clothes and literally "playing" the queen. Thus she provides an injection of vitality, of natural spontaneity, into the stuffy atmosphere of the court.

But inside this child there is a latent sensuality, whose emergence and effect is foreshadowed in a series of vivid gestures. When she first catches sight of the king, Rahel throws herself before him, clasping his foot, removes her jewelry and shawl, and prepares to sleep with her cheek resting on his knee. Alfons is obviously taken by her beauty, makes a lewd reference to her breasts, but finds himself confused by the initial encounter. It is not until he goes to her in the garden-house that his passions are fully aroused. He has erotic fantasies, depicting pale limbs reclining on soft cushions, and refers later to Rahel's fiery eyes and the voluptuous shape of her body (641). Throughout Act II Grillparzer conveys through imagery and symbolic episode in one of his most disturbing dramatic sequences the irrational and malignant nature of the passion that is engulfing him. Rahel is associated with witches and magic arts as she threatens to stick needles into Alfon's picture, and Alfons registers her threat physically in his own breast, as if she did have some supernatural hold over him. She is depicted caressing his picture and tempting it with sweet words, then as a voracious animal, who will suck his blood thirstily like a vampire. There is something demonic and elemental about Rahel, and her attraction is expressed in terms of supernatural influence again when she leaves a miniature of herself behind her as she departs to go home. Alfons finds it, it burns in his hand, and he does indeed feel as though he is in the grip of magic powers. But, as his friend Garceran realizes, there is no magic at work here in the literal sense of the word, only the magic of sexual desire, for this is Alfons's first genuinely sexual experience. In effect, nature is having its revenge for the neglect it has suffered during his earlier life.

But because we are concerned here with a purely physical passion, Rahel's hold over Alfons does not retain its original intensity. By the time we see them in Act III the affair is on the wane. Alfons is now impatient at Rahel's childish whims, he is determined to end the "game" he has been playing, and even permits Garceran to flirt with Rahel instead; she in turn welcomes this new lover as a change for the better.

It is in the light of these developments that Grillparzer has to motivate Rahel's murder, and this he does by returning to the political theme in real earnest. Despite his concentration on the love affair, Grillparzer never allows us to lose sight of the political situation altogether. We know that the Moors pose an immediate threat to the country's security, and Garceran repeatedly reminds the king that his place is with his army at the frontier. As a result, Alfons is caught in a conflict between his rising passion and his duties to his endangered country. What began as a harmless game turns into a serious dereliction of duty, which is how the affair is viewed by the nobles when they assemble to discuss the situation in Act IV. In this scene Grillparzer makes no attempt to portray a realistic conference involving discussion and argument as he had in *Ein Bruderzwist*. Here the nobles speak literally as one voice, that of Manrique, who is the only one to be given an identity and character. The rest have a purely symbolic function, assenting in silence to Manrique's words of wisdom, and suggesting that the representatives of the state are closing ranks. For Manrique, Rahel's seduction of Alfons has separated him from his people, so violating the order of the state; the country is leaderless at a time of danger. Manrique's attitude is echoed by the queen. She feels that Rahel has offended against the solemn law of marriage; she is a stain on the face of the earth, and must be removed from the king's side through death. Thus Manrique determines that if Alfons will not himself agree to send Rahel away, then the nobles will be forced to take the more extreme measure and execute her (1240-5). Rahel's fate is thus sealed in the ensuing interview between Alfons and the queen.

The presentation of the king's attitude at this stage represents one of Grillparzer's subtlest pieces of psychological realism, for though Alfons's passion for Rahel continues to diminish, his interest in her is not yet dead. He is full of remorse, admits his error, and can now take a more rational view of the "magic" which possessed him, recognizing it as something perfectly natural. He harps now on Rahel's faults, her cunning, vanity, and foolishness, and apparently agrees to Manrique's stipulation that she should be sent away (1445). It seems at this stage that Grillparzer is treating with psychological clarity and frankness the relatively "modern" theme of sexual aberration. Alfons has become disillusioned with the girl, and it even appears that his passing lapse could be deemed beneficial to his marriage. Initially at least, the queen welcomes his penitent attitude with greater warmth than she showed before, and Alfons is encouraged to conclude that they have both undergone a maturing experience. Yet Grillparzer suggests a continuing interest in Rahel through the fact that Alfons still wears her miniature around his neck, and this is enough for the queen to doubt the sincerity of his assurances.[34] He becomes exasperated, remembers again how prudish his queen is, then angrily denounces the nobles for daring to assemble in his absence. No wonder that when Manrique appears momentarily in the doorway the queen can only wring her hands in despair. This is a fatal gesture, and from it Manrique must conclude that Alfons has refused to agree to his stipulation. Shortly afterwards Manrique is seen briefly again, making for Retiro with Garceran to murder Rahel. While it is clear that Rahel still has a lingering fascination for Alfons, his exasperation and anger represent simply his ill-tempered reaction to the behavior of the queen and the nobles rather than any positive feeling for Rahel. Moreover, while Manrique's conclusion is explicable and defensible, it is not based on a full understanding of Alfons's state of mind. His situation is a delicate one and calls for understanding and patience, instead of which he encounters, because of the political crisis, an attitude that seems harshly uncompromising, moralistic, and intolerant. Rahel dies because the love affair is enacted against a specific political background, but even in this situation the justification for her death is not entirely proven, so that her swift and brutal sacrifice for the cause of the preservation of order in the state reflects badly upon her murderers.

Alfons's intial reaction to Rahel's death suggests that he too shares this view. In Act V he decides to have vengeance upon her murderers, even considers inciting his people to rebellion against them, and is now full of praise, not only for Rahel's beauty, but also for her spontaneity and naturalness, qualities which suggest on his part a conviction that for all her seductiveness she was indeed "innocent." At this stage of the tragedy we have the prospect of a revolution led by a heroic king against his ministers in the name of the state's innocent victim. But this is not to be. When the king goes to see Rahel's dead body, it is clear that she no longer attracts him; instead of recalling the ecstasies of the affair, he now thinks of his family and his people, and returns cleansed and purified to the fold. The king has washed his hands of Rahel. Her murderers are guilty, but so, too, as Manrique points out, is he; guilty not of having been responsible for Rahel's death, but for having deserted his duty by indulging in the affair in the first place. In this final act, then, the interest shifts from the possibilities of vengeance for Rahel to an atonement for the original blemish, and this Alfons hopes to achieve by leading his people to victory in battle. Such a victory will demonstrate that he is once again worthy of ruling over his peoples, and the affair with Rahel and her death can be put behind them all.

But the seemingly triumphant departure for the war is not the end of the play. After the king has left, Rahel's sister Esther expresses her bitter indignation at the mood of cheerful reconciliation now prevailing in the court, and she prophesies that the king will not be victorious, but will be defeated in the battle. It is then that he will think of Rahel with remorse:

> Wenn du emporschaust dann zum tauben Himmel,
> Dann wird das Bild des Opfers, das dir fiel,
> Nicht in der üppgen Schönheit, die dich lockte,
> Entstellt, verzerrt, wie sie dir ja mißfiel,
> Vor deine zagend bange Seele treten.
> Dann schlägst du wohl auch reuig an die Brust,
> Dann denkst du an die Jüdin von Toledo.   (1935–41)

(When you look up to the stony heavens, the image of the sacrifice that you made will appear before your fearful trembling soul. Not in her voluptuous beauty which seduced you, but disfigured and distorted, as she was when she no longer pleased you. Then indeed you will beat your breast in remorse, then you will think of the Jewess of Toledo.)

Clearly Esther is putting the blame for the tragic outcome on Alfons, but even at this late stage she modifies her attitude and forgives him, recognizing that all humans are guilty, united in sin and dependent on the forgiveness of God:

> Wir stehn gleich jenen in der Sünder Reihe.
> Verzeihn wir denn, damit uns Gott verzeihe.

(Like them, we stand in the line of sinners, so let us forgive, so that God will forgive us.)

In their suggestion of the imperfection of human nature, Esther's words form a fitting epilogue not only to this tragedy, but to Grillparzer's work as a whole, for though his characters are rarely presented as outright villains, their weaknesses and errors provide him with the main themes for his tragedies. In *Die Jüdin* Grillparzer offers a particularly cynical view of human behavior. The perfect Alfons and the childlike Rahel, both innocent in their own ways, become embroiled in a malignant passion, which, for the period of its duration, robs Alfons of all willpower, and totally diverts him from the path of duty. Furthermore, because the passion that Alfons experiences is purely physical lust, and not love, it is not imbued with the same intrinsic value immanent in the love of Hero for Leander, or of Edrita for Leon. Alfons's passion has no deeper significance than a passing desire for Rahel's body. His feelings for her are seen to wane, turn to disgust when she is dead, and with a gesture of self-purification, he shrugs off the influence that she had over him (see the stage direction following line 1812). The political figures of the play, who represent the interests of the state, Manrique, the nobles, the queen, and eventually the king himself, are also depicted in a less than favorable light. *Die Jüdin* is not a political play in the same sense as *Libussa* or *Ein Bruderzwist;* there are no speeches of political wisdom and no obvious references to contemporary events. Nevertheless, the love affair is set within a political context, and the tragic outcome is not without its political implications.

At the play's conclusion, the members of the court look forward to the restoration of a political order which, as we saw in Act I, requires of its ruler a total devotion to duty at the expense of personal feelings. The reestablishment of such an order is anticipated in a scene reminiscent of the finale of *Ein treuer Diener,* as Alfons introduces his little son to act as king in his absence at the battle. The tragedy has come full circle, with a symbol of innocence and purity at the helm, to await the return of Alfons himself, newly purified and ready to resume his original position. What is particularly unsatisfactory about this reversal to the original situation is that the order has been restored through the sacrifice of a victim, who at the moment of her death is possibly no longer guilty in the sense meant by her executors, i.e., of continuing to divert the king from the path of duty. The state's representatives are depicted with sympathy; both Manrique and the queen argue reasonably and from a position of principle, seeking not bloody revenge, but justice. But because we are afforded a considerable insight into the king's state of mind, they appear, in ignorance, to be taking unduly extreme and uncompromising measures. Had Grillparzer wished to suggest that the nobles were entirely justified in murdering Rahel, he would surely have had them do so when the love affair was at its height and the king was seen to be still completely under her spell. Indeed, simply because the affair is not presented as

a *grande passion* involving total commitment and promising eternal
devotion, we are made to feel that Rahel hardly deserves to die. Both
the murder of Rahel and the satisfaction felt at the prospect of a return
to order after her death cast a shadow over the later stages of this
tragedy, suggesting that the still liberal-minded Grillparzer shares
Esther's righteous indignation at the destruction of an innocent individual for the cause of the impersonal order of the state.[35] The political scenes of *Die Jüdin* were written in the aftermath of the 1848
Revolution, at a time when Grillparzer was no longer faced with the
prospect of political and social disorder. Now the concern of the
moderate liberal was that the new government under Francis Joseph
should not bring about a return to the iniquities of the pre-March
regime; such a concern finds its reflection in his treatment in *Die
Jüdin* of the reestablishment of a political order at the expense of
human life.

CHAPTER 6

Influence and Significance

I The Style

WITHIN the context of the history of German literature Grillparzer may be viewed primarily as a transitional figure, reflecting aspects of the German Classical period which preceded him, and revealing a tendency toward the Realism of the latter half of the nineteenth century.[1] As an Austrian he remained largely untouched by the contemporary German movements of Romanticism and *Jungdeutschland* (Young Germany). Indeed, he felt distinctly hostile to them. But this isolation was more than compensated for by his inheritance of a rich theatrical tradition which had developed in Vienna from the seventeenth century onward, and to the influence of which Grillparzer owes his reputation as one of the most effective of German dramatists. It was a tradition that he shared with contemporaries such as Raimund and Nestroy, and it was to continue later in the century in the plays of Ludwig Anzengruber and of the two preeminent dramatists at the turn of the century, Arthur Schnitzler and Hugo von Hofmannsthal. Hofmannsthal saw himself as a descendant of Grillparzer and repeatedly drew inspiration from Grillparzer's example, particularly in his mature years in the aftermath of the First World War. He shared Grillparzer's patriotic sentiments and regarded his predecessor as Austria's truly national poet, a spiritual link between the old Austria of Maria Theresa and the new Austria of Hofmannsthal's own generation, embodying what Hofmannsthal saw as the peculiarly Austrian qualities of moderation, sincerity, and tolerance.[2] Hofmannsthal also admired Grillparzer as a born dramatist, able to reflect the atmosphere and spirit of his fatherland through the sensuous medium of the stage.[3] Grillparzer was well aware of his indebtedness to his own cultural background and of his intimate ties with his native city. At the same time, he felt keenly his affinities with Goethe and Schiller, and the interesting combination of the Classical and the Viennese imbues his own dramatic style.

At the turn of the eighteenth and nineteenth centuries the tradition of the popular theater still flourished in Vienna's suburbs in
theaters such as the Theater an der Wien, the Leopoldstadttheater,
and the Josefstadttheater.[4] The most common forms were the popular comedy and the *Zauberstück*, a form of magical burlesque whose
scenes alternated between everyday reality and the supernatural
sphere of fairyland. These plays contained gay songs and dances,
reflecting the influence of the Viennese operatic tradition. The influence of Vienna's Baroque heritage, dating back to the late seventeenth century, was also strongly felt, with its elaborate operatic
stage, luxurious settings, splendid decorations, and ingenious stage
machinery. There was a strong local appeal, with comic characters
speaking in Viennese dialect and alluding constantly to the locality in
a dialogue replete with jokes and puns. But, because of censorship,
serious social, political, and religious themes were pursued only
superficially, and the reflection of Viennese life was not a realistic
one. Raimund's roots in this tradition were deep. He began as an
actor on the popular stage, and he enjoyed considerable success with
his *Zauberstücke* such as his famous *Der Bauer als Millionär* [The
Millionaire Peasant, 1826], but when he began to introduce more
serious tragic themes, as in *Die unheilbringende Zauberkrone* [The
Fatal Crown, 1829], he began to lose his popular appeal. In bridging
the gap between the popular theater and the Burgtheater,
Grillparzer went further than Raimund, who was never performed in
the Burgtheater in his own lifetime, but Grillparzer too found it
difficult to retain the favor of the public with his more sophisticated
style.

Grillparzer's own connections with the popular theater stem from
his visits in his early youth to the Leopoldstadttheater, and we have
already noticed its obvious influence on the dream sequence of *Der
Traum ein Leben* and on some of the early scenes of *Libussa*. The most
frequently mentioned aspect of his style which suggests popular
influence is his concern with the visual elements of drama. His
settings are not as lavish as those presented on the popular stage, but
some of his most memorable scenes, such as the arrival of the effer-
vescent Rahel among the staid courtiers in the royal garden of Toledo,
Ottokar's flamboyant display before his assembled court, the setting
for the opening scene of *Des Meeres und der Liebe Wellen*, possess an
intrinsic stage value and visual appeal of their own. His ability to mold
the total stage picture is seen to good effect even in *Ein Bruderzwist*,
which is arguably his least theatrical play. When the archdukes arrive
in the camp of the imperial army, they are greeted by Klesel against a

background of soldiers standing to attention. The characters then form individual groups. The archdukes cross to the opposite side of the stage; Klesel remains alone, ignored; Leopold discusses with Ramee his plans for recruiting an army in Passau; soldiers talk together of Don Cäsar's activities near the camp. These are all separate episodes, proceeding simultaneously, on which the audience eavesdrops in turn, until they are brought together in a climax with the announcement of the safe return from battle of Mathias, at which even the enigmatic Klesel cannot conceal his joy.

One of the best known features of Grillparzer's dramatic style is his use of visible stage properties such as the weapon in *Die Ahnfrau*; the rose, wreath, and lyre in *Sappho*; the shields in *König Ottokar*; the dove and priestly robe in *Des Meeres und der Liebe Wellen*. In this study we have also noted the striking use of gesture in the depiction of the behavior of Ottokar, Otto, and Erny (in *Ein treuer Diener*), Hero and Rahel. Through these means Grillparzer enhances the plasticity, the *Bildlichkeit* of his overall stage effect, but it is a characteristic feature of his style that such devices are not included for visual effect alone, but are integrated into the play as essential components of the dramatic action. The shields in *König Ottokar* and the dove and priestly robe in *Des Meeres und der Liebe Wellen* are used to provide both an anticipation of future events and a symbolic indication of the true nature of the central character. The fleece in *Das goldene Vließ* and the belt in *Libussa*, besides having a symbolic function, have their own role in furthering the action of these plays. The same is true of the king's picture and of Rahel's miniature in *Die Jüdin*. Gestures are used to provide an indication of a character's state of mind and are indeed often more eloquent than words. Those of Ottokar and Rudolf II in the scenes in which they are first displayed are used to establish for the audience a particular image of the hero. In the incident in which Ottokar hears of the result of the imperial election his gestures actually contradict his bold words and provide a penetrating insight into his state of mind. Through the stage directions Grillparzer provides frequent instructions to his actors, and it is clear from the concern that he betrays in letters and diary notes over the casting of roles, that he felt that the ability of the individual actor to interpret some of his more challenging portraits was vital for the success of his dramas. Several of his failures were in fact due to inadequate individual stage performances.

In the face of the success of the popular theater in the suburbs, an attempt was made in the late eighteenth century to establish a more refined style of theater in the Burgtheater, with an international repertoire. At first the attempt failed, but the appointment in 1814 of Josef Schreyvogel as artistic director provided a new impetus, and his company achieved a standard of excellence that earned for the Burgtheater a considerable reputation. Schreyvogel was steeped in the cultural ideals of the German Enlightenment and Classical period, was an admirer of the Greek dramatists, as well as of Shakespeare and Calderón, and stressed the moral role of the theater, praising dramatists such as Lessing and Kotzebue for their clarity and formal control. In particular, he felt hostile to the spectacular artificial effects cultivated in the popular theater and to the wild extravagances of the Romantics.[5] Both in his writings and personal advice Schreyvogel helped to broaden Grillparzer's cultural horizons and to foster his appreciation for the ideals of German Classicism. Certainly his influence may be detected in Grillparzer's choice of subject-matter and in some of the more superficial aspects of his style. Grillparzer's treatment of such themes as the problem of the artist, ambition, guilt, and duty, and his interest in Greek myth and historical material place him in the same tradition as the Classical Goethe and Schiller. *Sappho* and *Des Meeres und der Liebe Wellen* in particular possess the simplicity and symmetry of Goethe's Classical plays, and the predominant use of iambic blank verse is also a feature of the plays of German Classicism. Reminiscent of these, too, are the occasional monologues in Grillparzer's plays in which characters analyze their emotions (for example, *Sappho*, 792–857), and statements by characters such as the priest in *Des Meeres und der Liebe Wellen* which purport to have universal validity:

> Wer Taten-kräftig
> Ins rege Leben stürzt, wo Mensch den Menschen drängt,
> Er mag Gefahr mit blankem Schwerte suchen,
> Je härtrer Kampf, so rühmlicher der Sieg. (978–81)

(Whoever plunges energetically into the pressures of an active life, must seek danger with his naked sword, for the harder the battle, the more praiseworthy the victory.)

Although Grillparzer remained receptive to the techniques of the popular style, he incorporated the more popular aspects of his plays within a recognizably Classical framework.

Another aspect of Grillparzer's plays suggestive of higher aspirations than those toward a mere appeal to popular taste is his treatment

of characters. Although some of Grillparzer's characters are reminiscent of the caricatures or types of the popular stage, he is far better
known for his more subtle psychological studies, particularly of
female characters, and his famous *Seelenstudien*, or "studies of the
soul," constitute his own particular contribution to the history of
Viennese drama. At the same time his methods of portraying character and states of mind suggest a move away from the more
straightforward and direct methods of the Classicists. Grillparzer's
dramas introduce a new period of preoccupation with psychological
truth, to be pursued in the field of the drama by Friedrich Hebbel,
the Naturalists, and particularly by Arthur Schnitzler. Grillparzer is
indeed one of the first authors of the nineteenth century for whom
psychological study becomes a dramatic end in itself, and in his
occasional suggestions of unconscious motivation—for example, in
Erny of *Ein treuer Diener*—he has even been claimed to be a
forerunner of Freud. Grillparzer's concern for psychological verity is
most frequently referred to when attempts are made to claim him as
an early Realist, though it must be stressed that this concern stems in
particular from his admiration for Shakespeare, whom Grillparzer
studied at Schreyvogel's suggestion from 1817 on. Grillparzer was
most impressed with Shakespeare's ability to penetrate the depths of
human nature and to enter into the very souls of his characters (III,
643). He praised the characterization of Macbeth and Lady Macbeth
as representing typical male and female characteristics (III, 647), and
then later, in 1826, was intensely preoccupied with the characterization of Hamlet (III, 650–2). In Grillparzer's own plays the study of
Sappho's sexual frustration and jealousy, the analysis of the ill-fated
relationship between Jason and Medea, and the exposure of Ottokar's
essential weakness as a man provide early evidence of the importance
that he attached to characterization, and the studies of Otto and Erny,
Hero and Leander, Alfons and Rahel were to follow in his maturer
years.

In his monograph on Grillparzer's dramatic style, Joachim Kaiser
devotes a whole chapter to an analysis of Grillparzer's methods of
conveying the mental and emotional states of his characters.[6] He
mentions in particular those gestures denoting emotional stress, such
as the tears which Rudolf II sheds when he condemns his son to death
(*Ein Bruderzwist* 2186–8), and, more interestingly, gestures which
amount to a betrayal of feelings of which the character remains
unconscious. For example, in *Die Argonauten* Medea is apparently
unaware of the effect that Jason has had on her, and betrays her

emotions involuntarily by her physical collapse when she hears his voice (930). Characters may betray their emotions and preoccupations through swift changes of mind and attitude, sudden involuntary exclamations, interruptions, misunderstandings, moments of hesitation and confusion. Grillparzer favors an indirect revelation of feelings rather than a direct confession which identifies the precise nature of the emotion felt. The audience is permitted an insight into the character, is penetrating the outer mask, scrutinizing and analyzing the character's state of mind like a psychiatrist.

Despite the predominant use of a verse form employed by Goethe and Schiller in their Classical period, the language of Grillparzer's dramas suggests a tendency away from pure Classicism into a more realistic mode of expression. Analysts of his verse form have pointed to the prevalence of broken lines, interruptions and pauses in the flow of the dialogue, and a frequent lack of rhythmic stress, to suggest that although Grillparzer retains the bare bones of blank verse, many passages of dialogue have a distinctly prose-like quality, and are suggestive of the short, rapid exchanges of real conversation. His language is less declamatory and rhetorical than Schiller's, there is a notable lack of poetic embellishment, and his verse has been described as bare, undecorated, economical.[7] What poetic images there are tend to be drawn from the speaker's immediate environment and interests—the sea for Hero, the heavenly bodies, the Bible, the world of science and the arts for Rudolf II. Commentators have stressed the elliptical qualities of Grillparzer's language, involving the omission of auxiliary verbs ("was ich euch verweigert," "das vom Stein gedrückt"), and the elimination of inessential words which have only a grammatical function ("bis klar," "ich tat es, weil verfolgt," "wenn noch so spät").[8] This not only gives an impression of brevity and conciseness, but the omissions give added weight to the words and phrases carrying the sense, so facilitating comprehension for the audience. A good example is provided when Rudolf II hears that Mathias has been hailed as King of Hungary:

> Der Ungarn König? Nun: voraus bezeichnet,
> Nachfolger etwa; ob auch das zur Zeit
> Nicht sicher noch, abhängig von gar vielem.   (1382–4)

([As] King of Hungary? Certainly [he is] designated [for this office], perhaps [as my] successor; though at this moment even this is not certain, [and is] dependent on many things.)

Here the essentials of Rudolf's thought processes are transmitted successively to the audience without the complexities of connecting words. Grillparzer's sentences tend to be short, but where longer sentences occur in the lengthy speeches of characters such as the two Rudolfs or the priest in *Des Meeres und der Liebe Wellen,* the sentence structure itself tends to be straightforward. Sentences are divided into easily digestible units, which often correspond to the single lines of the text. E. E. Papst suggests that Grillparzer writes in a paratactic or "additive" style, preferring the use of successive main clauses, or nouns and phrases placed in apposition to each other rather than of complex subordinate clauses.[9] Another feature of Grillparzer's style is his adaptation of German word order to the requirements of drama, involving the placing of verbs used in subordinate clauses as early as possible ("weil Ruhe war in meiner Steiermark," "daß abgetan der Zwist und die Zerwürfnis"). Such deviations from normal prose usage are not intended to produce a more poetic or heightened style, but to give greater emphasis to the sense-bearing words in the interests of clarity. Indeed, they approximate to everyday speech patterns, and so contribute to the colloquial impression made by his frequent use of the exclamations, abbreviations, and contractions of ordinary conversation ("Ei!," "Du liebe Zeit!," "müd," "sitz," "obs," "andre," "leicht" for "vielleicht," and countless others). The speeches of Naukleros in Act II of *Des Meeres und der Liebe Wellen* provide a constant stream of examples.

But although certain aspects of Grillparzer's style point the way to a more realistic dramatic form than that employed by the German Classicists, it cannot be claimed that his plays anticipate the principles of German Naturalism. Despite his insistence on psychological truth, the complete psychological and sociological motivation of the Naturalists, with their emphasis on hereditary and environmental factors, is absent in Grillparzer. Grillparzer was himself hostile to the excessive realism of the writers of *Jungdeutschland,* as well as to the fashionable *Bürgerliches Trauerspiel* ("Bourgeois Tragedy"). At most it could be claimed that Grillparzer was part of a trend toward Realism, a trend to which he personally felt unsympathetic, and it is possible that he was not even aware of contributing to it. If anything, he was closer to the "Poetic Realism" or "Artistic Realism," as defined by Otto Ludwig, than to the harsh Realism of Georg Büchner, Gerhart Hauptmann, and Arno Holz.[10] If Grillparzer absorbed elements of the popular theater and the Classical stage, he also steered a middle course between Classicism and Realism. His mid-position

may be illustrated best by his comments on Goethe, for though he
admired Goethe for his formal qualities, he found his dialogues
unnatural and not well related to their situation (III, 765). Goethe's
later works in particular suffered, he felt, from artificiality, especially
the second part of *Faust*, which he criticized for being too fantastic,
incoherent, and confusing (G IV, 214). Goethe's earlier works, on the
other hand, were too realistic for Grillparzer's taste.[11]

Grillparzer did not develop an aesthetic theory in so comprehensive or definitive a form as Schiller, and he was in any case mistrustful
of aesthetic theorizing, yet his various notes and unpublished essays
do suggest a view of art based on principles close to the Classical ideals
of Goethe and Schiller. Fundamental to Grillparzer's aesthetic principles is his belief that the work of art should be an object of beauty,
and though he felt that the concept of beauty itself defies *a priori*
definition, he felt justified in an attempt to analyze its effect. In this
respect Grillparzer's principles, however vaguely stated, are reminiscent of Schiller's. The effect of beauty is one of pleasure, which,
though derived from sensuous impressions, is a heightened one,
transcending purely sensual delight and involving a sublimation of
one's whole self. The contemplation of beauty lifts the onlooker out of
the narrow confines of his own existence, affords him a feeling of
wholeness and unity of being, in which the sensual and spiritual sides
of his nature are in harmony (see particularly III, 216–7, 228). But if
Grillparzer was implying that the work of art should present some
heightened reality with a spiritual as well as a sensuous appeal, the
main pillar of his beliefs is his insistence that the work should nevertheless retain an intimate relationship with the real world and con-
form to the laws of nature. A work of art should not constitute a slavish
reproduction of reality; indeed, no individual art form can reproduce
nature in precise terms. At the same time, it should possess a recognizable affinity with the world of reality. A drama, for example, must
not present characters or events the like of which could not possibly
exist or take place in reality (III, 217–9). If art should possess the
quality of beauty, it should also have truth. The artist will select,
emphasize, refine, but he will do so from the basis of the world as
known to himself and his audience, so as to represent a modified or
subjective version of the truth (III, 223–4). Grillparzer goes into no
details as to the laws governing this processing of reality, but he does
lay considerable stress on the importance of the artist's technique.

In his essay written in 1834 on contemporary German drama,
Ueber den gegenwärtigen Zustand der dramatischen Kunst in

Deutschland [*On the Present State of Drama in Germany*, III, 686–91], Grillparzer maintains that the fundamental task of the dramatist is to present the illusion of actuality (*die Supposition von einer Gegenwart*), which is obviously subject to the technical limitations of the theater, but which, for the duration of the performance, the spectator is prepared to accept as a postulated reality (*eine vorausgesetzte Wirklichkeit*). Such an illusion may be achieved through a convincing motivation of events, through the establishment of a chain of cause and effect whereby the connection between event and character may be readily recognized. In a draft for an essay on drama written in 1820, *Ueber das Wesen des Dramas* [*On the Essence of Drama*], Grillparzer had already insisted that *strenge Kausalität* ("strict causality") was a principle fundamental to the essence of drama (III, 301), and in his affirmation of this principle he comes closest to the critical tenets of Lessing. The creation of such a causal chain confers on it an internal logic of its own, thereby appealing to the spectator's reason and convincing him of the reality of what he sees. Grillparzer's own psychological studies are more subtle and complex than this simple system might allow, but as G. A. Wells has suggested, the principle of causality is sustained consistently in all his plays as a fundamental structural feature.[12] In this respect, then, Grillparzer's concern for psychological truth does indeed suggest a tendency to Realism, but to impress the spectator with the *beauty* of the stage reality the dramatist clearly has to appeal to qualities other than reason, and in his essay of 1834 Grillparzer mentions imagination (*Phantasie*), feeling (*Gefühl*) and sense-perception (*Empfindung*) as forces that must also be brought into play. For Grillparzer, a work of art is not an entity that can simply be thought out (*gedacht*), it must also be felt with the senses (*empfunden*), it must be given life and form. A drama in particular must have visual qualities (*Anschaulichkeit*), plasticity (*Körperlichkeit*), and sense impressions are vitally important for a full appreciation of its beauty. The beauty of a drama does not simply reside in the poetry of its language, though this may be an important contributory factor (III, 861), but in its total appeal. In his plays Grillparzer aims primarily at psychological truth, a logical internal organization, and a visual appeal, and through the perfection of these qualities he attempts to adhere to his fundamental principles of truth and beauty.

Like much of the aesthetic theorizing of the period, Grillparzer's ideas are only set out in the vaguest terms, and, apart from his stipulation of causality, he can give no precise guidelines as to *how* the qualities of beauty and truth may be achieved. Grillparzer recognizes that successful drama depends in the final analysis on a dramatist's natural talent, and it was Grillparzer's own talent which so impressed his successor, Hugo von Hofmannsthal. For Hofmannsthal, Grillparzer excelled as a composer, in particular as an inventor of moving and theatrically effective individual situations. He had a gift for matching characters of widely differing temperaments—he cites the example of Bishop Gregor and the kitchen-boy Leon—and of incorporating into the same play such different types of character as saints, seers, and lovers. [13] It was as natural, or naive, dramatists that Grillparzer likewise admired Shakespeare and Lope de Vega. The influence of the theater of the Spanish Golden Age is often mentioned in connection with the more visual elements in Grillparzer's dramatic style. He praised the sensual aspects of Spanish drama, the pictorial and lively qualities of its scenes, its emphasis on action or "play" (Spiel), rather than on discussion or reflection. In particular, he was drawn to the nonintellectual approach of Lope de Vega, whose plays appeared to develop as "spontaneously as nature itself" (III, 415). Lope wrote with a seemingly artless and enchanting elegance, his work was imbued with a healthy realism, and his natural presentation of character rivalled Shakespeare's. He also shared with Shakespeare a desire to incorporate as much of the action as possible on the stage in a series of loosely connected episodes, rather than rely heavily on reports and descriptions, a principle which Grillparzer readily followed. In his pursuit of naturalness and visual beauty Grillparzer was more in tune with Shakespeare and the Spanish dramatists than with the German Classicists, and of his own Austrian contemporaries he found much to admire in the "truth-to-nature" (Naturwahrheit) of the dramas of Raimund and J. C. von Zedlitz. [14] It is in the spiritual affinity between the Spanish and the Austrian artistic temperament that the key to an understanding of Grillparzer's dramatic art is to be found.

One of the sadder anomalies in the history of the theater is that, for all their widely acknowledged theatrical qualities, Grillparzer's plays should not have enjoyed more stage success either in his lifetime or since. Not that he could be called a neglected dramatist. Since his death his plays have appeared regularly in the repertoire of the Burgtheater in Vienna, where Der Traum ein Leben has been performed most frequently. In Germany his plays have been most produced in Dresden, Berlin, and Hamburg, and several of his works have been filmed and broadcast. Nevertheless, they have never been outstandingly popular. Abroad, the situation has been even worse, and Arthur Burkhard has demonstrated, for example, that there is only a sparse record of Grillparzer performances in the United States, and indeed a "deplorable showing in England."[15] Several possible reasons have been advanced to explain Grillparzer's unexpected lack of popularity. In his own day it was undoubtedly his attempt to combine the more elevated form of German Classical tragedy with popular elements. In leaning too much toward the former he failed to provide the entertainment required even by the Burgtheater audience, and found himself remorselessly parodied by lesser dramatists. In recent years, according to Norbert Fürst, he has suffered with the decline in the theater world of the importance of the actor and the corresponding rise of that of the director.[16] But it is also possible that despite his subtle characterization and tendencies toward a more realistic dramatic style, audiences still regard him simply as a later, less extreme, and therefore less "pure" exponent of Classicism than the more illustrious Goethe and Schiller. Given the nature of the subject-matter of many of his tragedies, it is reasonable to suppose that audiences expect to be confronted with high tragedy on the grand scale. Yet with the absence of characters of heroic stature and their prevailing mood of melancholy and resignation, his plays are lacking in the tragic grandeur of some of Schiller's later tragedies. Grillparzer is too steeped in tradition to be instantly recognizable as the forerunner of new tendencies in the theater, but at the same time too independent a figure to satisfy the lovers of Weimar Classicism.

II *The Content*

In view of the value that Grillparzer himself placed on the technical skill of the dramatist and on the achievement of an immediate, sensuous appeal to the theater audience, it may seem surprising that considerable critical attention has been focused not on the theatrical qualities of his plays, but on their intellectual content. The plays have been investigated in terms of their moral or political implications, and conclusions regarding Grillparzer's own philosophy of life have been drawn from the values which he appears to uphold, and from the aspects of human behavior which, by implication, he condemns. Given the themes he treats, this process is inevitable, and any full-scale study of his works must at least attempt to come to terms with their content. It has, for example, become fashionable to divide his plays into groups according to their subject-matter, and recent classifications have included the plays of action and ambition, the historical or political plays, the problem of the artist, and duty and love, so cutting across the chronological development of the dramatist.[17] His works have been interpreted as allegories of the conflict between the artist's mission and life, or, in more general terms, between duty and desire.[18] The tragic conflict common to his plays has been described as that between "the timeless realm of eternal forms and the temporal physical realm of living experience," neither of which offer total fulfillment to the human personality.[19] Arguments have been advanced to suggest that his plays represent, in various forms, the surrender of personal integrity and purity to the destructive passions of love and ambition (Gerhard Fricke), or the fundamental tragic dilemma deriving from the inevitability of man's participation in an active life (Ilse Münch).

In his early years Grillparzer was himself vigorously opposed to the notion that the function of art was to express some single idea. In his view the appeal of the work of art was essentially to the senses, and no true artist proceeded with the simple intention of expressing in his work some general philosophical principle. Grillparzer also felt that the assumption that works of art should have a moral purpose was in fact the greatest enemy of true art. The theater in particular was not a corrective institution. On the other hand, Grillparzer could write in 1820 that a play should at least represent the functioning of the eternal laws of morality against those who transgress. This does not necessarily mean that the purpose of tragedy is to bring about the moral improvement of the spectator. But drama should represent the glorification of the eternal moral law (die Verherrlichung des Rechts, III, 303). This comment is obviously relevant to a superficial understanding of Das goldene Vließ and König Ottokar, both of which conclude with the feeling that the hero is getting his just deserts. By 1837 Grillparzer was even admitting that a work of art may be based on a "fundamental idea," though he insisted that this idea must be given life and concrete form (III, 287). It must be understood immediately via the senses, "felt" through one's sense perceptions (Empfindung), without the necessity for lengthy intellectual reflection (III, 227–8). Grillparzer is suggesting that a work of art may at least give an immediate, sensory impression of an idea, even of an interpretation of life, but it must not be too obviously the product of intellectual thinking. Writing in 1848, Grillparzer criticized contemporary German writers specifically on the grounds that, under the influence of the speculative philosophy of Hegel, they had proceeded with the assumption that every work of art should represent some philosophical idea (III, 719–20). Hegel had encouraged the Germans to presume that they could discover the key to the mystery of the universe, and this was reflected in their literature, which Grillparzer found doctrinaire and intellectually presumptuous. In particular, he singled out Friedrich Hebbel as a "thinker" rather than an "artist," and felt that of his own contemporaries only Heinrich Heine appealed directly to the reader's *Empfindung*, while Austrian writers alone still retained the warmth and naturalness of true art.

Critics agree that of the oeuvres of the major figures of the nineteenth century, Grillparzer's works have the least admixture of ideas, but it is nevertheless true that there is a moralistic strain in the early tragedies, and that, of the later works, both *Libussa* and *Ein Bruderzwist* contain long speculative speeches. If Grillparzer did not presume to set forth in his plays any systematized philosophy, this does not mean that he himself was incapable of intellectual thought, nor that his ideas might not have found their reflection in his creative works.

Grillparzer's tendency to round his plays off with a judgment passed upon the behavior of the central character (Rudolf's assessment of Ottokar or Esther's condemnation of Alfons) suggests that a fundamental idea or moral precept does underlie the action. Some of his plays, such as *Das goldene Vließ* and *Der Traum ein Leben* end with the pronouncement of a general moral, while others, such as *Ein treuer Diener* and *Weh dem, der lügt!*, have a clear framework structure in which a character is set a particular task, encounters problems as he attempts to carry it out, and is then judged as to the degree of his success. Such features have prompted Joachim Kaiser to point to the bow-like structure of Grillparzer's plays (*Bogenform*), the tendency for characters to embark from a specific situation on a course of action, only to return chastened and disillusioned to the original position.[20] This is a structural principle which most obviously underlies the careers of Ottokar and Rustan, and which Grillparzer took from the popular theater of his day. Raimund's *Der Bauer als Millionär*, for example, is also based on the simple, proverbial truth that pride goes before a fall, and the central character learns the bitter lesson of the futility of the pursuit of fame and fortune. The theme of the futility of earthly happiness, which may be represented so appropriately by the framework structure, was also a common one in the drama of the Spanish Baroque from Calderón onward. It would, however, be misleading to suggest that Grillparzer's plays can all be conveniently "summed up" as representations of such a simple moral. Underlying his tragedies is a profound awareness of a human predisposition to error, an inability to achieve success or preserve innocence in so many different kinds of activity, from Sappho's desire for happiness in love to Emperor Rudolf's attempts to preserve peace. Many of his plays close in an atmosphere of resignation and with a sense of guilt, expressed in the early tragedies by Medea's "Suffer!. . . Endure!. . . Atone!" and culminating in Mathias's "Mea maxima culpa" and Esther's "We stand like them in the line of sinners." The endings of Grillparzer's tragedies lack the sense of relief derived from the recovery of lost innocence which is a feature of the Baroque and popular dramas; and the sense of guilt and sin conveyed particularly in *Ein Bruderzwist* and *Die Jüdin* is not inspired by the activities of one particular wayward individual, but is a general one in which all the characters share.

The prevalence of error and sin in Grillparzer's tragedies is such that for some critics they transmit a powerful impression of the inevitability of human guilt, which for Joseph Sprengler is even suggestive of the force of necessity and for Ernst Busch of the fatefulness of human life.[21] These reactions imply that Grillparzer's dramas are imbued with a sense of fatality usually associated with ancient tragedy, an interpretation which is apparently supported by his own comments on the nature of drama. In 1820 he wrote that the modern force in drama is not freedom, but necessity, and that the feeling aroused by tragedy is one of pain at the evils of life (III, 300–1). These views seem to be at variance with the essentially optimistic principles of the Enlightenment and with Christian doctrine, both of which insisted on man's essential freedom and autonomy. Moreover, they seem to contradict the contemporary view that in contrast to Greek tragedy, "modern" tragedy should stress the role of character and the human will.[22] Certainly Grillparzer's early fate-tragedy *Die Ahnfrau* contains a strong sense of fatality and a suggestion of supernatural influence, and even in the tragedies which are more rationally based, an atmosphere suggesting the inevitability of disaster is generated which, as Ulrich Fülleborn has pointed out, gives the impression that some indeterminate power is in control of events.[23] For example, the frequent use of warnings ("Believe me, Ottokar, you stand at the abyss!," *König Ottokar* 637), dire prophecies ("She'll regret it, and sooner than she imagines!," *Libussa* 465), and forebodings ("I told you so! This can only lead to disaster!," *Die Jüdin* 659) help to create a sense of doom or of impending retribution.

After *Die Ahnfrau*, however, the sense of fatality conveyed in Grillparzer's plays in no way carries with it the implication that an external force either initiates or controls the fatal chain of events. Even in *Das goldene Vließ* the powers attributed to the fleece itself are really to be found in the intentions and emotions of the characters, and in other plays the basis for catastrophe exists, for example, in the passion and jealousy of Sappho, the grandiose ambition of Ottokar, the naive error of 'Iero. If many of Grillparzer's characters seem to be moving inevitably toward catastrophe, in some cases blindly, in others knowingly, they are simply reaping the consequences of some initial decision or powerful emotion. As is often alleged, Grillparzer's characters do indeed tend to become prisoners of the developing situation, but it is usually a situation of their own making and stems from their own characters and emotions. One thinks immediately of Sappho's decision to seek the love of Phaon, Jason's to seek the fleece, Hero's to enter the temple, and Rustan's dream-experience of the consequences of his decision to seek his fortune. And if in *König Ottokar* there is no active decision on the part of the hero to seek the imperial crown, he is swept along by his own ambition and sense of personal grandeur. Even in the case of Bancbanus and Rudolf II, who are initially more passive and simply find themselves cast in roles for which they are unsuited, a major contributory factor to their ills is their own temperament. The fate of Grillparzer's characters lies essentially in their own natures, and the force that operates upon them is an inner, psychological one. In *Das goldene Vließ* it is a seemingly independent force that takes arbitrary hold of the human being (*Die Argonauten* 1012–14); in *Des Meeres und der Liebe Wellen*, it can so alter a character's will and direction that it appears to occasion a complete change of personality (1181–91); in *Die Jüdin* it seems to be endowed with magic force, robbing the character of all willpower. Yet in the final analysis it is a force that comes from within.

Occasionally in his plays Grillparzer depicts situations in which characters seem to lose control of events, to the extent that the results of their actions go far beyond their original intentions. In *Ein treuer Diener*, for example, Count Peter hurls his dagger into the darkness in the direction of the escaping Otto, but to his horror kills the queen by mistake. In a strikingly similar incident in *Ein Bruderzwist* Don Cäsar fires his pistol in sheer rage through the open door of the room into which Lukrezia has fled, and then expresses his horror at the awful consequences by throwing himself onto his knees, covering his face with his hands. Episodes such as these suggest to some critics that the source of tragedy in Grillparzer's plays lies in the inability of the human being to control his actions, in the very nature of activity itself, as though activity were a force independent of the characters.[24] Yet this loss of self-control still has its roots in human nature, and in the incidents just mentioned it has a psychological cause in the impetuosity and fiery temperaments of the characters.

Grillparzer's concentration on the internal psychological processes of his characters suggests in itself that in his view the tragedy of life is deeply rooted in human nature, a view which distinguishes him from other nineteenth-century dramatists, who tend to stress the role of external forces such as political or social factors (Büchner), the inevitability of the grand historical process (Hebbel), the influence of heredity and environment (Hauptmann and the Naturalists). At the same time, it is his apparently pessimistic presentation of human nature that divides him sharply from the eighteenth-century optimists, from the faith of the Rationalists in human reason, the glorification of the powerful personality of the Storm and Stress dramatists, the assertion of spiritual freedom found at the close of Schiller's late Classical dramas. The Grillparzer hero also tends to be a weaker character than the Shakespearian or Schillerian hero, and heroic qualities in the traditional sense are largely absent from Grillparzer's works. Grillparzer tends to expose the limitations and weaknesses of his characters. Most obviously, there are the would-be heroic types, Ottokar and Rustan, who face humiliation and are "unmasked," or cut down to size. Similar to them are Jason, the confident adventurer who ends a broken man; Duke Otto, the libertine who suffers a nervous collapse; and Archduke Mathias, whose ambitious feelings dissolve once he comes to power. Equally prominent are those who are overcome by strong emotions, such as King Alfons, and notably the female characters Sappho, whose public image is tarnished as a result, Medea, who betrays her family against her will, and Hero, who quickly abandons her resolution. Then there is a third type of "anti-hero" exemplified by Bancbanus and Rudolf II, essentially good men with high principles, who are called to tasks that are beyond them. But these latter two characters in particular are treated sympathetically, and Grillparzer emphasizes their admirable qualities as well as their weaknesses. When one considers also the sympathetic treatment of the love relationships in *Des Meeres und der Liebe Wellen, Weh dem, der lügt!* and *Libussa*, it is clear that Grillparzer's attitude to human nature grew warmer as he himself matured, as indicated notably by the statement at the close of *Libussa* of an ultimate faith in the return of humanitarian values to society as a whole.

Despite the moralistic tone of some of the early works, there are, with the possible exception of Zawisch, no true villains in Grillparzer's works, for even the worst are depicted as people who are originally virtuous and who go astray unintentionally through weakness of will, through an inability to control their emotions, or through misguided principles.[25] In his notes on drama written in 1820 Grillparzer maintains that true tragedy occurs when a human being recognizes the futility of life (*das Nichtige des Irdischen*) and perceives the dangers to which even the best of mortals may succumb (*die Gefahren sieht, welchen der Beste ausgesetzt ist und oft unterliegt*, III, 303). Certainly the words *das Nichtige des Irdischen* suggest on Grillparzer's part an unrelievedly pessimistic attitude toward all human affairs, but the remaining words of his comment are indicative of a sympathetic and tolerant attitude. Indeed, he goes on to claim that the most appropriate emotions at the close of a tragedy are *Menschenliebe* and *Duldsamkeit* ("a love for mankind" and "tolerance").

The moralistic strain prevalent in Grillparzer's early tragedies, and his tendency to close his tragedies with confessions of guilt and sin, have led to the assumption that a fundamental moral law lies at the root of Grillparzer's works, a law which possesses absolute validity and against which the conduct of the characters is judged.[26] Moreover, the recurrent presence of a religious theme suggests that this moral law is divinely inspired, and that a God-given order and system of values is being affirmed in contrast to the imperfect world of human affairs.[27] This is certainly the import of the early speeches of Rudolf II. Rudolf I also asserts at the close of *König Ottokar* that it is the hand of God that has deemed it right to punish the hero for his arrogance, and Esther suggests at the conclusion of *Die Jüdin* that God will be the ultimate judge of the behavior of all. The tragedies based on Greek legends are also enacted against a background of divine authority. Yet it would do little justice either to their dramatic qualities or to the subtleties of their characterization to treat Grillparzer's plays as mere religious allegories. It should also be borne in mind that Grillparzer was not himself an orthodox believer. In his early years he lapsed from his Catholic heritage and renounced traditional Christian beliefs. He was an admirer of Voltaire, became skeptical of religious doctrine and of any systematic statement of faith, and it is doubtful whether he ever genuinely believed that the will of God could be perceived in any way.[28] What remained was a humble reverence for a distant and inscrutable God, a vague and uncertain awareness of an order of perfection unhappily beyond the reach of ordinary mortals. Grillparzer's all too keen perception of human inadequacies and his occasional bouts of bitter despair over earthly affairs quickly began to predominate over his religious faith. It is, therefore, reasonable to assume that his plays were neither intended as embodiments of Christian doctrine, nor that they preach modes of behavior derived from the moral tenets of any orthodox faith. At most, the religious theme of his plays represents a convenient framework within which the behavior of his characters may be judged.

Nevertheless, there are characters in his plays who, either through calling or inclination, profess an affinity with the divine, and who uphold values derived from their own religious beliefs. The emperor Rudolf I, for example, feels that his role is something akin to a religious mission, imposed on him by God. In devoting himself selflessly to the preservation of law and order in the empire, he is in effect upholding God's law. Similar sentiments are voiced by Rudolf II, who regards it as his task to ensure that the empire itself should be a reflection of the heavenly order. Largely because of the attitudes displayed by these characters critics have seen in Grillparzer's plays an expression of his own veneration of the law, and of his respect for the traditions and values of his cultural and political heritage, in particular a glorification of the order of the state as an institution having absolute value over the interests of the individual. Yet this is a value that is scarcely upheld with any consistency in his works. From other plays it is possible to deduce that Grillparzer was well aware that the ideal of an unselfish devotion to the interests of the state might occasionally involve an intolerable human sacrifice. Both Bancbanus and King Alfons discover this in their different ways. Moreover, those who act in good faith in the name of the state may sometimes appear to be harsh and inhumane, and both Primislaus and the nobles of *Die Jüdin* come in for heavy criticism from characters who are outraged by their behavior. In these tragedies Grillparzer's reverence for law and order is seen to be tempered by his love of humanity and respect for the rights of the individual, and a political skepticism is revealed which sets him apart from many of his contemporaries.

If the political attitudes of the two Rudolfs have been too readily identified as Grillparzer's own, another character who has been taken as his author's mouthpiece is the priest of *Des Meeres und der Liebe*

Wellen. He, too, derives his principles from his religious views, devoting himself single-mindedly to a life of private spiritual communion with the gods. But it is his eulogy of the ideal of *Sammlung* that has done most to identify him as Grillparzer's spokesman. As a representative of the contemplative life of the seer, he has been associated closely with Bishop Gregor of *Weh dem, der lügt!* and with the sisters Kascha and Tetka of *Libussa,* and more loosely with the poetess Sappho, for *Sammlung* was for Grillparzer essentially an artistic ideal. The recurrent presence in Grillparzer's plays of characters who remain apart from what could be regarded as the normal world of activity has led to interpretations of his plays in terms of a fundamental duality of the active and contemplative life. Moreover, because participation in "life" in Grillparzer's works invariably seems to involve characters in guilt and eventual misery, it is tempting to assume that devotion to a life of contemplation must necessarily represent a contrasting positive ideal. The ideal of contemplation and of a withdrawal from the affairs of the world is central to the philosophy of Schopenhauer, whom Grillparzer read and admired as early as 1819. Yet just as the ideal of a selfless devotion to the state is not always treated by Grillparzer with unqualified enthusiasm, so too does the contemplative life have its shortcomings. In particular the female characters Sappho, Hero, and Libussa find that it necessitates a sacrifice of their more natural inclinations. Grillparzer's characters are not faced with a simple choice between contemplation and activity, "art" and "life," "duty" and "desire." Invariably the choice is presented in terms of a dilemma. The characters who indulge in the fullness of life may indeed suffer pain and lose their purity, but many who attempt to withdraw from life altogether find that they would do so only at the cost of real experience and of fulfillment as a complete human being. Of the characters who seem more satisfied by their life of contemplation, the priest seems uncompromisingly inhumane, Libussa's sisters cold and unattractive, and Bishop Gregor seems remote from the practical realities of life.

It is Grillparzer's skeptical presentation of ideals which further distinguishes him from the optimism and certainties of the Classical age. The codes of life to which his more idealistic characters adhere are either unsatisfactory or inadequate, and testify to Grillparzer's doubts concerning man's ability to achieve perfection in his modes of living or institutions.

Grillparzer's honest, if sympathetic, presentation of human failings and his skeptical treatment of ideals stamp him as one of the foremost exponents of nineteenth-century pessimism. It has been generally recognized that his plays are imbued with a strong sense of the tragedy of life, which finds expression through a variety of means. Most obviously, his plays present a record of failure on the part of so many characters to achieve their hopes and intentions. Sappho fails to find happiness in love with Phaon, and she suffers a destructive jealous passion. Ottokar's hopes of gaining the imperial crown are dashed, and he has to endure the most painful humiliation. Libussa fails to establish her ideal community, Rudolf II to preserve peace. Perhaps the most poignant reaction to a character's failure comes from King Andreas, who returns to his country to find that not only has Bancbanus failed to keep the peace, but his own queen has perished in his absence:

> Bancban, Bancban, wie hast du mich getäuscht
> Um mein Vertrauen, das ich auf dich gewendet!
>   (*Ein treuer Diener* 1874f.)

(Bancban, Bancban, how you have disappointed me and cheated me of the trust which I placed in you!).

In his plays Grillparzer also generates a pessimistic atmosphere through the statements of his characters. Very occasionally there are brief reflections on the lot of mankind, as when Phaon considers the miserable condition of human beings and the contrast between bright hopes and their fulfillment (*Sappho* 484–6). More frequently come warnings of approaching disaster. Ottokar and Hero are warned that they stand on the edge of the abyss, the "Abgrund," and expressions of fear and forebodings are found particularly in *Das goldene Vließ* and *Die Jüdin*.

Grillparzer's plays also tend to close on an appropriately somber note, and here too contrasts may be seen with the conclusions of eighteenth-century tragedies. Just as Grillparzer avoids a positive or enthusiastic presentation of the strong, the powerful, and the heroic, none of his tragedies closes with any sense of Storm and Stress defiance against hostile forces. Lacking, too, is the Schillerian moral triumph of the human spirit over the senses, and there is no assertion of the possibilities of freedom from the misfortunes of life. Indeed, Grillparzer contested the view that freedom should be the main force in modern drama, and wrote that the spiritual upsurge that accompanies the victory of freedom is completely out of tune with the nature of tragedy (III, 302–3). Grillparzer's tragedies tend to close in an atmosphere of resignation or of retrospective sadness as characters look back over events or review their mistakes. Mathias provides the most memorable example, and in the earlier tragedies Sappho is reconciled to the fact that the gods have not permitted her to drink a full share of life's pleasures; Medea is prepared to bear on her shoulders the awful guilt she has incurred; and Ottokar is full of remorse over his behavior as ruler. Bancbanus is more defensive about his conduct, but refuses to accept any reward for his fidelity. His final attitude is one of humility and melancholy, as he retires to his estates to await the day when his body will be buried beside that of his wife. The closing sequences of two of Grillparzer's tragedies contain more bitter moments. In *Des Meeres und der Liebe Wellen* Ianthe turns on the priest and enjoins him to look at the corpses of the two lovers, the tragic consequences of his actions, while in *Die Jüdin* Esther voices her indignation at the attitude of Alfons and his courtiers. Yet this final tragedy of Grillparzer's eventually ends on a note of reconciliation and humility, as Esther forgives Alfons and includes herself among the sinful. The atmosphere is one of humble and tolerant resignation, one which may well reflect Grillparzer's own attitude toward human nature. This attitude is illustrated, too, at the close of *Der Traum ein Leben* when Massud, despite his reservations concerning Rustan's character, is persuaded to give his blessing to the love-match between Rustan and his daughter with a reluctantly approving *seis!* ("so be it!").

Grillparzer's pessimism is essentially a product of his own temperament and of a close observation of his fellow-men, and does not represent an adherence to any philosophical system. Yet it places him in a line of development between Kleist at the beginning of the century and the Naturalists at the end. He does not share Hebbel's conviction of the inevitability of the progress of mankind, but nevertheless does not exhibit consistently the bleak despair of Georg Büchner. Despite his obvious awareness of human failings, he was still capable of creating essentially noble characters such as Bancbanus and Rudolf II, of depicting the natural charm and innocence of Melitta, Hero, and Edrita, of writing the idyllic opening scene of *Libussa*. It is Libussa herself who eventually affirms the essential goodness of man, and expresses her faith in the return to society of the virtues of brotherly love and humility, fundamental humanitarian ideals which are central also to the works of Grillparzer's Austrian contemporary Adalbert Stifter.

Though he had scant regard for Stifter as a writer, Grillparzer shared with him a detestation for many of the political and social trends of their time, in particular for the development of materialistic and self-interested attitudes engendered by scientific and technological progress. Both responded with equal disquiet to the events of 1848, and both have been regarded as essentially conservative figures on the cultural scene. Yet, although both men were susceptible to pessimistic moods, they exhibit through their sympathetic portrayal of many of their characters their own faith in humanity and love of their fellowmen. Stifter's pious clergyman in his story *Kalkstein* [Limestone, 1853] was, for example, inspired by Grillparzer's portrait of the honest, decent and essentially noble musician in *Der arme Spielmann*. Grillparzer's pessimism is apparent in so many aspects of his works, yet it is not an exclusively dominant force in them, and particularly in the works of his middle and later periods there are several alleviating features.

Nevertheless, because of the melancholy tone of his works and the mood of resignation which tends to prevail at their conclusion, Grillparzer has been regarded as a typical representative of the Biedermeier period, and has been associated with contemporary writers such as Eduard Mörike, Jeremias Gotthelf, Annette von Droste-Hülshoff, Ernst von Feuchtersleben, as well as with Stifter himself. In particular, Grillparzer's critical treatment of human passions and activities has been singled out as a Biedermeier feature, as has been his skeptical presentation of powerful and would-be heroic personalities. Other aspects of his work that have been noted in this connection are his avoidance of violent scenes and strident outbursts of passion, the muted and restrained tone of his plays, his predilection for quiet and gentle endings to acts and scenes.

Yet if the tendency has been to use "Biedermeier" to identify lesser writers of the period or writers who are considered either conservative or essentially unpolitical, Grillparzer's relationship to the concept is somewhat problematic. Certainly, as 1848 approached, he showed a fear of violent political and social upheaval, but his later works have their political implications, and are at least suggestive of his own moderate liberalism. Moreover, if the ideal of a withdrawal from the affairs of the world into the idyll of domestic tranquillity is a Biedermeier ideal, then only *Der Traum ein Leben* provides an explicit advocation of it, and in other works the ideal of contemplation or retirement is treated more skeptically. Grillparzer was well aware of the destructive qualities of human passion, but his middle and later works suggest that the vital forces cannot easily be suppressed and certainly not ignored. As Jost Hermand has suggested, any attempt to establish absolutely his relationship to the so-called Biedermeier writers of the period only serves to underline the lonely position that Grillparzer occupied among his contemporaries.[29]

Notes and References

Chapter One

1. For an easily digestible account of this period, see Ilse Barea, *Vienna: Legend and Reality* (London: Secker and Warburg, 1967), pp. 111–88.
2. *Wiener Biedermeier: Begegnungen und Erlebnisse* (Vienna: Bergland, 1960), pp. 106–26.
3. *Vienna: The Image of a Culture in Decline* (London: Macmillan, 1938), p. 206.
4. J. P. Stern, "Grillparzer's Vienna," *German Studies* (London, 1962), p. 181.
5. *The Fall of the House of Habsburg* (London: Longmans, 1963), p. 20.
6. The term has been variously discussed, for example, by E. E. Papst, *Grillparzer: "Des Meeres und der Liebe Wellen"* (London, 1967), pp. 12–16; W. E. Yates, *Grillparzer* (Cambridge, 1972), pp. 130–31, 158–61.
7. See H. Hoff and I. Cermak, *Grillparzer* (Vienna, 1961), pp. 10–20.
8. *Wiener Biedermeier*, p. 108.
9. Caroline Pichler's memoirs (1844, quoted in the Hanser edition of Grillparzer, IV, 892); Bauernfeld's diary entry for 28 February 1827, also quoted in Hanser IV, 925–26.
10. Douglas Yates, *Franz Grillparzer* (Oxford, 1964), finds little justification for regarding Grillparzer as a manic depressive. In his opinion Grillparzer, as a creative artist, was "at all times predisposed to take himself to task and grow depressed because of his recurrent unproductivity" (p. 114).
11. Letter to K. F. Zelter, 11 October 1826, quoted in Hanser IV, 924.
12. *Travel Stories* (1836), quoted in Hanser, IV, 937–38.
13. Hoff and Cermak (p. 63) suggest that it was the strong influence upon him of his mother's personality that made him so hesitant in this respect. In effect, he feared that sexual relations with certain women would destoy the image of his mother which he found in them.
14. In May 1826 Grillparzer wrote in his diary: "It was not really on grounds of virtue [that I decided *not* to make love to the girl], the decision was produced by what was perhaps merely an aesthetic, artistic enjoyment of her purity. It was this which held me back from accomplishing what all my thoughts and feelings were urging me almost irresistibly to do" (IV, 400).
15. J. Nadler, *Franz Grillparzer* (Vienna, 1952), pp. 118–19.
16. For example, in a letter to E. von Schenk, 28 January 1827 (IV, 779).

Chapter Two

1. E. R. McDonald, *"Die Ahnfrau*: Franz Grillparzers Metapher des schicksalhaften Lebens,"* Maske und Kothurn* 18 (1972): 3–22.
2. As argued by F. Lorenz, "Franz Grillparzers *Ahnfrau*: Eine Schicksalstragödie," *Grillparzer–Forum Forchtenstein 1968* (Heidelberg: Stiehm, 1969), pp. 79–99.
3. Grillparzer's original, unaltered version appears in SB I, 1, 149–256; the final version, which Grillparzer published in 1844, usually called the "stage version," appears in SB I, 1, 9–148 and in Hanser I, 607–708. Critics wishing to demonstrate the effect of Schreyvogel's advice usually compare these two versions.
4. The use of the ghost as a dramatic device has been explored more fully by R. K. Angress, "Das Gespenst in Grillparzers *Ahnfrau,*" *German Quarterly* 45 (1972): 606–19.
5. This is explored especially well by E. R. McDonald.
6. See McDonald, pp. 6–7.
7. Nadler, p. 137.
8. Herbert Kraft, *Das Schicksalsdrama* (Tübingen: Niemeyer, 1974), pp. 68–83); McDonald, p. 14.
9. *Grillparzers dramatischer Stil* (Munich, 1961), pp. 95–100.
10. For example, W. E. Yates (p. 72) interprets her death as symbolic of the acceptance of the artist's need to cut himself off from life.
11. A similar interpretation of her suicide is suggested by Ilse Münch, *Die Tragik in Drama und Persönlichkeit Franz Grillparzers* (Berlin, 1931), p. 33; and G. A. Wells, *The Plays of Grillparzer* (London, 1969), pp. 34–45.
12. For example, W. E. Yates, pp. 65–72.
13. H. Politzer, *Franz Grillparzer* (Vienna, 1972), p. 130.
14. C. S. Baker, "Unifying Imagery Patterns in Grillparzer's *Das goldene Vlieβ,*" *Modern Language Notes* 89 (1974): 392–403.
15. See Baker, pp. 394–98; T. C. Dunham, "Symbolism in Grillparzer's *Das goldene Vlieβ,*" *PMLA* 75 (1960): 75–82.
16. O. E. Lessing, *Grillparzer und das neue Drama* (Munich: Piper, 1905), p. 33; on the other hand W. E. Yates (p. 95) maintains that Medea's crimes are such inhuman atrocities that she can scarcely be regarded as a suitable vehicle for the expression of the moral of the play.
17. "Symbolism in Grillparzer's *Das goldene Vlieβ,*" p. 82.
18. "Grillparzer's Ottokar," *Germanic Review* 39 (1964): 261.
19. W. E. Yates (p. 99) writes: "That Ottokar, like Sappho, is shown as falling short of an absolute ideal, and that this is the *moral* core of his tragedy, is in keeping with a recurrent tendency in Grillparzer's dramatic work."
20. Edward McInnes, "*König Ottokar* and Grillparzer's Conception of Historical Drama," *Essays on Grillparzer,* edited by Thompson and Ward (Hull, 1978), pp. 25–35, discusses Ottokar's political errors.
21. See W. Naumann, "*König Ottokars Glück und Ende,*" *Das deutsche Drama,* edited by von Wiese (Düsseldorf, 1969), I, 413–14.

22. Underlying Silz's interpretation is a strong suggestion that sexual problems lie at the root of Ottokar's behavior.

Chapter Three

1. Commentators who criticize the behavior of Bancbanus and his presentation as a tragic hero include, notably, Friedrich Gundolf, "Franz Grillparzer," *JbFDtHochst.*, 1931, pp. 57–59; and J. Müller, *Grillparzers Menschenauffassung* (Weimar: Böhlaus, 1934), pp. 61–67.

2. In a detailed instruction concerning the interpretation of the role to the actor Löwe (IV, 783–85).

3. D. Yates, p. 128.

4. Most recently by P. Lattmann, *Franz Grillparzer: Untersuchungen zu seinem Drama 'Ein treuer Diener seines Herrn'* (Zurich: Juris, 1971), pp. 65–66.

5. "Zum Problem des Tragischen in Grillparzers *Treuem Diener*," *German Quarterly* 31 (1958): 10.

6. Papst (p. 39) writes: "This sickness unto death [i.e., love], to which both the play's heroes fall victim, is thus revealed . . . as the true agent of tragedy."

7. Notably Papst, pp. 43–44.

8. M. E. Atkinson, "Grillparzer's Use of Symbol and Image in *Des Meeres und der Liebe Wellen*," *German Life and Letters* NS 4 (1950–51), 274.

9. Ed., *Der Traum ein Leben* (Cambridge, 1968), pp. 24–27.

10. "Grillparzer's Drama *Der Traum ein Leben*," *Zeitschrift für Deutschkunde* 54 (1940): 49–65.

11. *Grillparzer* (Kronberg, 1976), p. 200.

12. At this point the original version of the play, published in 1840, emphasized the intellectual problem, as Edrita asserts that a man may lie through his behavior, even though his words may be strictly truthful: "Es lügt der Mensch in Worten nicht allein, auch mit der Tat." (Quoted in the notes to the text in II, 1251–2.) The new version has been taken from the corrections that Grillparzer made on his own copy of the 1840 edition, which was found in his library after his death. It places greater emphasis on the love element and is now the more generally accepted version. Wells (pp. 28–29) alone dismisses the love theme as a minor element and interprets the play essentially in terms of the original version.

Chapter Four

1. In this connection comparisons have been made between Grillparzer's poetry and Byron's, which is also inspired by "a kind of passionate thinking." See W. E. Yates, *Grillparzer*, p. 156.

2. *Die deutsche Literatur im 19. Jahrhundert* (Stuttgart: Kröner, 1969), p. 174.

152 FRANZ GRILLPARZER

3. W. Paulsen, "Grillparzers Erzählkunst," *Germanic Review* 19 (1944): 59–68.
4. See R. H. Lawson, "The Starost's daughter Elga in Grillparzer's *Das Kloster bei Sendomir*," *Modern Austrian Literature* I (1968): 31–37.
5. R. Brinkmann, "*Der arme Spielmann*," *Wirklichkeit und Illusion* (Tübingen, 1957), pp. 87–145, argues that despite Grillparzer's attempts to provide an objective, truthful depiction of the musician, he can only achieve a subjective account, whether from the narrator's or from the musician's own perspective.
6. A point made by Benno von Wiese, "*Der arme Spielmann*," *Die deutsche Novelle* (Düsseldorf, 1969), I, 147.
7. E. E. Papst, ed., *Der arme Spielmann* (London, 1960), p. xxvi.
8. J. P. Stern, *Re-interpretations* (London, 1964), writes: "What emerges as the sole positive value is . . . not the art which he has so faithfully 'practised' for a lifetime. . . . What emerges at the end . . . is the intention and the pure heart alone, the disembodied good will as the absolute and only value" (p. 72).
9. As argued by Papst, *Spielmann*, p. xx.

Chapter Five

1. Especially by P. Kuranda, "Grillparzer und die Politik des Vormärzes," *Jb. der Grillparzergesellschaft* 28 (1926): 4–5.
2. Notably by R. Alewyn, "Grillparzer und die Restauration," *Publications of the English Goethe Society* 12 (1937): 1–18; and W. E. Yates, *Grillparzer*, pp. 223–36.
3. *Grillparzer*, p. 223.
4. As claimed by Alewyn, "Grillparzer und die Restauration," p. 9.
5. W. Carr, *A History of Germany 1815–1945* (London: Arnold, 1969), p. 12.
6. T. S. Hamerow, *Restoration, Revolution, Reaction: Economics and Politics in Germany 1815–1871* (Princeton: Princeton University Press, 1958), pp. 65–66, 89, 119, 129.
7. Hamerow, pp. 65–66.
8. Nadler (pp. 271–72) refers to his "politische Wandlung" at the time, and describes his poem "Der Reichstag" as a retraction of all his previous views.
9. His reactions to the revolution are recorded in four *Aufrufe* (Exhortations), addressed to the revolutionaries, though unpublished at the time; quoted in III, 1040–48.
10. R. J. Rath, *The Viennese Revolution of 1848* (New York: Greenwood, 1969), p. 218.
11. Rath, p. 243.
12. See G. Stein, *The Inspiration Motif in the Works of Franz Grillparzer* (The Hague, 1955), pp. 155–87.

13. Gundolf (p. 84) emphasizes the play's lack of unity.
14. Analyzed fully by T. C. Dunham, "The Circle Image in Grillparzer's *Libussa*," *Germanic Review* 36 (1961): 125–36.
15. John Denison Barlow, *The Dramatic Structure of Grillparzer's 'Libussa,'* Diss. New York University, 1967.
16. As argued by Dunham, *Libussa*, p. 131.
17. As does Münch, pp. 91–98.
18. See especially Stein, p. 192.
19. Initially O. E. Lessing, pp. 122–31.
20. *Franz Grillparzer*, p. 324.
21. *Grillparzer*, p. 262.
22. Many critics, including W. E. Yates (p. 263), place less emphasis on the optimistic conclusion to her prophecy.
23. By W. Naumann, *Grillparzer* (Stuttgart, 1967), p. 47.
24. For example, by E. E. Papst, "Franz Grillparzer," *German Men of Letters* (London, 1961), I, 115.
25. As stressed by Naumann, *Grillparzer*, p. 48.
26. Including Benno von Wiese, *Die deutsche Tragödie von Lessing bis Hebbel*, 7th ed. (Hamburg: Hoffmann and Campe, 1967), pp. 440–44.
27. As argued by E. Mason, "A New Look at Grillparzer's *Bruderzwist*," *German Life and Letters* 25 (1971–2), 108.
28. "Grillparzers *Bruderzwist in Habsburg*," *Literatur und Kritik* no. 61 (February 1972), 19–20.
29. "Grabbe and the Development of Historical Drama," *German Life and Letters* NS 32 (1979), 111. McInnes writes that the actions of Rudolf are "eclipsed by the relentless momentum of impersonal historical processes."
30. *The Plays of Grillparzer*, pp. 121–22.
31. *Franz Grillparzer*, pp. 362–69.
32. "A New Look at Grillparzer's *Bruderzwist*," p. 113.
33. Several critics comment on the unsatisfactory nature of the initial situation, among them Münch (p. 86) and Wells (pp. 127–28).
34. As A. D. Klarmann, "Grillparzer und die Moderne," *Die Neue Rundschau* 67 (1956): 149, maintains, it is not clear in the text whether the king is really prepared to renounce Rahel.
35. Critics who take a similar view of the play's tragic outcome include Gundolf (p. 77), who argues that feelings of humanity have been sacrificed for the cause of the state; and G. Fricke, *Studien und Interpretationen* (Frankfurt/M, 1956), p. 279, who emphasizes the fact that the state has only been preserved through an atrocity.

Chapter Six

1. See W. N. B. Mullan, "Grillparzer and the Realist Tradition," *Forum for Modern Language Studies* 13 (1977): 122–35.

2. "Grillparzers Politisches Vermächtnis" (1915), *Gesammelte Werke* (Frankfurt/M: Fischer, 1964), *Prosa* III, 256–58.

3. "Rede auf Grillparzer" (1922), *Werke, Prosa* IV, 118–19.

4. For an account of the Viennese popular theater, see J. Michalski *Ferdinand Raimund* (New York: Twayne, 1968), pp. 19–47; and Dorothy Prohaska, *Raimund and Vienna* (Cambridge: Cambridge University Press, 1970).

5. W. E. Yates, "Josef Schreyvogel, Critic and Mentor: An Inquiry into Aspects of Schreyvogel's Influence on Grillparzer," *Publications of the English Goethe Society* 44 (1973–4): 83–108.

6. *Grillparzers dramatischer Stil,* pp. 32–72.

7. Hofmannsthal, "Rede auf Grillparzer," p. 121.

8. A comprehensive analysis of Grillparzer's sentence structure has been undertaken by Albert Fries, *Intime Beobachtungen zu Grillparzers Stil und Versbau* (Berlin: Ebering, 1922); Hans Gmür, *Dramatische und theatralische Stilelemente in Grillparzers Dramen,* Diss. Zurich, 1956, pp. 50–54, also comments on the elliptical qualities of Grillparzer's style.

9. Ed., *Des Meeres und der Liebe Wellen,* p. 22.

10. Mullan, p. 134, n. 26.

11. F. D. Horvay, "Goethe and Grillparzer," *Germanic Review* 25 (1950): 91.

12. *The Plays of Grillparzer,* p. 15.

13. "Rede auf Grillparzer," pp. 118–25.

14. See particularly his comments on Raimund's *Der Alpenkönig und der Menschenfeind* (III, 830–32).

15. *Franz Grillparzer in England and America* (Vienna: Bergland, 1961), p. 31.

16. *Grillparzer auf der Bühne* (Vienna: Minutius, 1958), p. 275.

17. See particularly the studies by G. A. Wells and W. E. Yates.

18. Notably by D. Yates.

19. Papst, *Grillparzer,* p. 107.

20. *Grillparzers dramatischer Stil,* 109–12.

21. J. Sprengler, *Grillparzer: Der Tragiker der Schuld* (Stuttgart: Bürger, 1947); Ernst Busch, "Wesen und Ursprung von Grillparzers Idee des Tragischen," *Euphorion* 40 (1939): 257–76.

22. See, for example, Goethe's essay "Shakespeare und kein Ende," *Gedenkausgabe der Werke, Briefe und Gespräche,* 24 vols. (Zurich: Artemis, 1948ff.), XIV, 761–62.

23. *Das dramatische Geschehen im Werk Franz Grillparzers* (Munich, 1966), pp. 101, 125.

24. See, for example, R. Mühler, "Grillparzer und der deutsche Idealismus," *Wissenschaft und Weltbild* I, No. 1 (1948), p. 64; E. Staiger, *Meisterwerke Deutscher Sprache* (Zurich: Atlantis, 1948), p. 172.

25. Fritz Strich, *Franz Grillparzers Aesthetik* (Berlin: Duncker, 1905), p. 189.

26. G. Baumann, *Franz Grillparzer* (Frankfurt/M, 1966), p. 30, writes: "Underlying all is a fundamental ethical feeling, a moral norm."

27. See particularly Erich Hock, *Franz Grillparzer: Besinnung auf Humanität* (Hamburg: Hoffmann and Campe, 1949), p. 81; and Fricke, p. 282; W. E. Yates, *Grillparzer*, p. 100, writes of a diary note of 1820: "In a way that is highly characteristic of the moral emphasis in Grillparzer's work, the idea of God means a supreme standard of law and of right."

28. Colin Walker, "The Light of the Gods in *Des Meeres und der Liebe Wellen*," *Essays on Grillparzer*, edited by Thompson and Ward (Hull, 1978), p. 38.

29. *Die literarische Formenwelt des Biedermeiers* (Giessen, Schmitz: 1958), p. 195.

Selected Bibliography

The bibliography includes only a small selection of the numerous critical studies of Grillparzer and his works. It has been prepared with the needs of the English-speaking reader in mind and is limited to the most important accessible studies. Readers requiring further bibliographical information are referred to Joachim Müller, *Franz Grillparzer*, Sammlung Metzler, No. 31 (Stuttgart: Metzler, 1963), and to Annalisa Viviani, *Grillparzer Kommentar*, 2 vols. (Munich: Winkler, 1972).

PRIMARY SOURCES

A. Grillparzer's Works

Franz Grillparzer. Edited by K. Pörnbacher, Dichter über Dichtungen. Munich: Heimeran, 1970. Assembles Grillparzer's writings on his own works from a variety of sources.

Grillparzers Gespräche und die Charakteristiken seiner Persönlichkeit durch die Zeitgenossen. Edited by A. Sauer. 7 vols. Vienna: Verlag des Literarischen Vereins, 1904–41.

Sämtliche Werke, Ausgewählte Briefe, Gespräche und Berichte. Edited by P. Frank and K. Pörnbacher. 4 vols. Munich: Hanser, 1960–64.

Sämtliche Werke: Historisch-kritische Gesamtausgabe. Edited by A. Sauer and R. Backmann. 3 divisions, 42 vols. Vienna: Gerlach and Wiedling [from 1916 Schroll], 1909–48.

B. Annotated Editions

Der arme Spielmann and Prose Selections. Edited by E. E. Papst. London: Nelson, 1960. Informative introduction; interprets the work in terms of the dilemma facing the artist in his task of mediating between the ideal and the real.

Der Traum ein Leben. Edited by W. E. Yates. Cambridge: Cambridge University Press, 1968. Full introduction; relates the play to the Viennese popular theater.

Der Traum ein Leben. Edited by W. E. Yuill. London: Nelson, 1955. Introduction has short, standard interpretation.

Des Meeres und der Liebe Wellen. Edited by Roy C. Cowen. Waltham, Mass.: Blaisdell, 1969. General introduction; little interpretive comment on text; helpful linguistic notes.

Des Meeres und der Liebe Wellen. Edited by Douglas Yates. Oxford: Blackwell, 1960. Introduction largely based on chapter in Yates's book on G; full notes; first published 1947.

156

Die Jüdin von Toledo. Edited by G. A. Wells. London: Pergamon, 1969. Very short introduction; helpful explanatory notes.

König Ottokars Glück und Ende. Edited by Lionel H. C. Thomas. Oxford: Blackwell, 1963. Full and scholarly introduction.

Sappho. Edited by Keith Spalding. London: Macmillan, 1965. Brief introduction has good analysis of Sappho's character and motives.

C. Translations

Franz Grillparzer: Plays on Classical Themes. Translated by Samuel Solomon. New York: Random House, 1969.

Franz Grillparzer: The Poor Musician. Translated by J. F. Hargreaves and J. G. Cumming in *German Narrative Prose,* edited by E. J. Engel, I, pp. 191–229. London: Wolff, 1965.

The Ancestress. Translated by Hermann Louis Spahr. Hapeville, Georgia: Tyler, 1938

The following have been translated by Henry H. Stevens, and published in Yarmouth Port, Mass., by the Register Press: *A Dream is Life* (1946). *Hero and Leander* (1938). *King Ottocar, his Rise and Fall* (1938). *Libussa* (1941). *Thou Shalt not Lie* (1939).

The following have been translated by Arthur Burkhard, and published in Yarmouth Port, Mass., by the Register Press: *A Faithful Servant of his Master* (1941). *Family Strife in Hapsburg* (1940). *Hero and Leander* (1962). *King Ottocar, His Rise and Fall* (1962). *Medea* (1941; 3rd rev. ed. 1956). *Sappho* (1953). *The Guest Friend and The Argonauts* (1942). *The Jewess of Toledo* (1953).

More information on translations can be found in Arthur Burkhard, *Franz Grillparzer in England and America,* Osterreich-Reihe, Nos. 134–36, [Vienna: Bergland, 1961].

SECONDARY SOURCES

A. In English

ANGRESS, R. K. *"Weh dem, der lügt!:* Grillparzer and the Avoidance of Tragedy." *Modern Language Review* 66 (1971): 355–64. Examines the play in terms of the contrast between primitive and civilized societies; good analysis of Leon's development.

ATKINSON, MARGARET E. "Grillparzer's Use of Symbol and Image in *Des Meeres und der Liebe Wellen." German Life and Letters* NS 4 (1950–1): 261–77. Intricate but sensitive analysis.

BAKER, CHRISTA SUTTNER. "Structure and Imagery in Grillparzer's *Sappho." Germanic Review* 48 (1973): 44–55. This study demonstrates the close interrelationship of the acts of the play and shows that Sappho finally resumes her image as an artist.

————."Unifying Imagery Patterns in Grillparzer's *Das goldene Vließ.*" *Modern Language Notes* 89 (1974): 392–403.

BLACKALL, E. A. "*Die Jüdin von Toledo.*" *German Studies Presented to W. H. Bruford*, pp. 193–206. London: Harrap, 1962. Interprets the play in terms of a contrast between dream and reality.

COWEN, ROY C. "The tragedy of *Die Jüdin von Toledo.*" *German Quarterly* 37 (1964): 39–53. Concentrates on the figure of Rahel; interprets the play as a tragedy of misplaced trust.

DUNHAM, T. C. "The Circle Image in Grillparzer's *Libussa.*" *Germanic Review* 36 (1961): 125–36.

————. "Symbolism in Grillparzer's *Das goldene Vließ.*" *PMLA* 75 (1960): 75–82. Argues that the trilogy's symbolic structure assists psychological insight into the characters.

ELLIS, JOHN M. "Grillparzer: *Der arme Spielmann.*" In Ellis, *Narration in the German Novelle: Theory and Interpretation.* Anglica Germanica, Ser. 2, No. 7, pp. 113–35. Cambridge: Cambridge University Press, 1974. An original interpretation, concentrating on the unpleasant characteristics of the narrator and representing the theme as the relationship of artistic integrity to efficiency.

KRISPYN, EGBERT. "The Fiasco of *Weh dem, der lügt!.*" *German Life and Letters* NS 25 (1971–2): 201–9. Blames the failure on political and social circumstances and on the presentation of Leon as a comic character.

————. "Grillparzer's Tragedy *Die Jüdin von Toledo.*" *Modern Language Review* 60 (1965): 405–15. Views the play as an allegory of the Fall, then as a victory of Duty over Desire.

MASON, EVE. "A New Look at Grillparzer's *Bruderzwist.*" *German Life and Letters* NS 25 (1971–2): 102–15. An original critical interpretation of Rudolf's character and behavior.

MORRIS, I. V. "The *Ahnfrau* Controversy." *Modern Language Review* 62 (1967): 284–91. An informative account.

MULLAN, W. N. B. "Grillparzer and the Realist Tradition." *Forum for Modern Language Studies* 13 (1977): 122–35. Presents Grillparzer as a transitional figure; analyzes his aesthetic theories.

PAPST, E. E. "Franz Grillparzer." In *German Men of Letters: Twelve Literary Essays*, edited by Alex Natan, I, pp. 99–120. London: Wolff, 1961. A good introduction, interpreting Grillparzer's works essentially in terms of the dualism of *Sammlung* and *Leben.*

————. *Grillparzer: Des Meeres und der Liebe Wellen.* Studies in German Literature, No. 9. London: Arnold, 1967. An ingenious study, presenting *Sammlung* as the ideal, love as the destructive force.

PEACOCK, RONALD, "Franz Grillparzer." In Peacock, *The Poet in the Theater*, pp. 39–53. New York: Harcourt and Brace, 1946. Stresses the theatrical qualities of G's plays and his attention to psychological detail.

SILZ, WALTER. "Grillparzer's Ottokar." *Germanic Review* 39 (1964): 241–61. Penetrating analysis of Ottokar's character.

STEIN, GISELA. *The Inspiration Motif in the Works of Franz Grillparzer, with special consideration of 'Libussa'*. The Hague: Nijhoff, 1955.

STERN, J. P. "Beyond the Common Indication: Grillparzer." In Stern, *Re-Interpretations: Seven Studies in Nineteenth Century Literature*, pp. 42–77. London: Thames and Hudson, 1964. On *Der arme Spielmann*; stresses the moral purity of the hero.

―――. "Grillparzer's Vienna." *German Studies presented to W. H. Bruford*, pp. 176–92. London: Harrap, 1962. A wide-ranging exploration of the intellectual atmosphere of the city.

SWALES, MARTIN W. "Grillparzer: *Der arme Spielmann*." In Swales, *The German 'Novelle,'* pp. 114–32. Princeton: Princeton University Press, 1977. Stresses the ambivalent presentation of the musician.

THOMPSON, BRUCE. *A Sense of Irony: An Examination of the Tragedies of Franz Grillparzer*. Literaturwissenschaftliche Texte, Theorie und Kritik, No. 4. Frankfurt/M: Lang, 1976. Examines irony as a feature of G's tragedies and dramatic style.

THOMPSON, BRUCE and WARD, MARK G., eds. *Essays on Grillparzer*. New German Studies Monographs, No. 5. Hull: New German Studies, 1978. Includes essays on *König Ottokar*, *Des Meeres und der Liebe Wellen*, *Der Traum ein Leben*, *Weh dem, der lügt!*, and the 1848 Revolution.

WELLS, G. A. *The Plays of Grillparzer*. London: Pergamon, 1969. A useful and clear account, with particular reference to dramatic effectiveness, characterization, and theory of tragedy.

YATES, DOUGLAS. *Franz Grillparzer: A Critical Biography*. Oxford: Blackwell, 1946; rpt. 1964. A detailed analysis of works up to *Des Meeres und der Liebe Wellen* in the light of G's personal life and problems, mainly in terms of the conflict between life and art. Second volume of this study was not completed.

YATES, W. E. *Grillparzer: A Critical Introduction*. Cambridge: Cambridge University Press, 1972. A full treatment of G's life and works, along traditional lines; works discussed in thematic groups, for example art, ambition, duty and love, politics and culture.

B. In German

BACKMANN, REINHOLD. "Grillparzer als Revolutionär." *Euphorion* 32 (1931): 476–525. A convincing study of G's liberalism, referring in detail to his diaries and poetry.

BAUMANN, GERHARD. *Franz Grillparzer: Dichtung und österreichische Geistesverfassung*. Frankfurt: Athenäum, 1966. A revision of his earlier work on G published in 1954; regards G's Austrian heritage as the key to his personality and works, stressing particularly his ambivalent attitude toward ideals and life and the melancholy tone of his works.

BRINKMANN, RICHARD. "*Der arme Spielmann*: Der Einbruch der Subjektivität." In Brinkmann, *Wirklichkeit und Illusion*, pp. 87–145. Tübingen: Niemeyer, 1957.

160 FRANZ GRILLPARZER

ENZINGER, MORIZ. "Franz Grillparzer und das Wiener Volkstheater." *Grillparzer-Studien*, edited by Oskar Katann, pp. 9–39. Vienna: Gerlach and Wiedling, 1924. An analysis of the Baroque and popular elements in Grillparzer's plays.

FRICKE, GERHARD. "Wesen und Wandel des Tragischen bei Grillparzer." In Fricke, *Studien und Interpretationen*, pp. 264–84. Frankfurt/M: Menck, 1956. A philosophical interpretation of G's works as representing the inescapable destructive forces of life and reflecting the disillusionment of the age.

FÜLLEBORN, ULRICH. *Das dramatische Geschehen im Werk Franz Grillparzers: Ein Beitrag zur Epochenbestimmung der deutschen Dichtung im 19. Jahrhundert.* Munich: Fink, 1966. A stimulating study which attempts to establish G as an early Realist through an analysis of the complex relationship between deeds and events in his works.

GUNDOLF, FRIEDRICH. "Franz Grillparzer." In *Jahrbuch des Freien Deutschen Hochstifts*, pp. 9–93. Frankfurt/M: Niemeyer 1931. A notorious essay decrying G as an outmoded imitator of the Classical style; regards G's works in a negative light as testifying to G's own weakness of will and melancholy disposition.

HOCK, ERICH. "Grillparzers Drama *Der Traum ein Leben.*" *Zeitschrift für Deutschkunde* 54 (1940): 49–65.

HOFF, HANS, and CERMAK, IDA. *Grillparzer: Versuch einer Pathographie.* Oesterreich-Reihe, Nos. 152–3. Vienna: Bergland, 1961. A detailed exploration of G's problematic personality.

KAISER, JOACHIM. *Grillparzers dramatischer Stil.* Munich: Hanser, 1961. A valuable analysis of G's verse form, methods of characterization, and of the dialogue and structure of his plays, suggesting his originality and individuality.

KLARMANN, ADOLF D. "Grillparzer und die Moderne." *Die Neue Rundschau* 67 (1956): 137–52. Sees G as a "modern" author mainly because of his attention to psychological detail and interest in complex personalities; aligns him with Schnitzler, Bahr, and Freud.

MÜNCH, ILSE. *Die Tragik in Drama und Persönlichkeit Franz Grillparzers.* Neue Forschung, No. 11. Berlin: Junker, 1931. One of the best of the earlier studies of G, stressing the susceptibility of G's characters to internal conflict and G's ambivalent attitude toward the division between the active and contemplative spheres of existence.

NADLER, JOSEF. *Franz Grillparzer.* Vienna: Bergland, 1952. The most comprehensive critical biography of G; first published 1948.

NAUMANN, WALTER. *Grillparzer: Das dichterische Werk.* Stuttgart: Kohlhammer, 1967. First published 1956; a study of particular themes in G's works, such as "appearance and reality," "judgment," "time"; treats also G's relationship with Goethe and the Spanish drama.

POLITZER, HEINZ. *Franz Grillparzer oder das abgründige Biedermeier.* Vienna: Molden, 1972. An admirable study displaying a penetrating insight into G's personality, and offering original and stimulating interpretations of his works.

ŠKREB, ZDENKO. *Grillparzer: Eine Einführung in das dramatische Werk.* Kronberg/Ts: Scriptor, 1976. Analyzes G's views on art and on other writers; pinpoints the more optimistic elements in G's plays and stresses his love of humanity.

STAIGER, EMIL. "Grillparzer: *König Ottokars Glück und Ende.*" In Staiger, *Meisterwerke deutscher Sprache aus dem 19. Jahrhundert,* pp. 165–87. Zurich: Atlantis, 1948. A sensitive and sympathetic interpretation of Ottokar's character.

WIESE, BENNO von. "Franz Grillparzer: *Der arme Spielmann.*" In von Wiese, *Die deutsche Novelle von Goethe bis Kafka.* 10th ed., I, 134–53. Düsseldorf: Bagel, 1969. First published 1956.

————, ed. *Das deutsche Drama vom Barock bis zur Gegenwart.* 5th ed., Vol. I. Düsseldorf: Bagel, 1969. First published 1958; includes essays on *König Ottokar* (by Walter Naumann), *Libussa* (by Erich Hock), *Ein Bruderzwist* (by Gerhard Baumann).

Index

Akademie der Wissenschaften, 18
Alker, Ernst, 86
Altmütter, Georg, 22, 23
Anacreontic lyric, 80
Anzengruber, Ludwig, 127
Auersperg, Count Anton Alexander ("Anastasius Grün"), 12, 85, 86, 97
Austria (political and social situation), 11–13, 84–85, 95–99, 127–28

Baroque, 47, 55, 128, 139
Bauernfeld, Eduard von, 11, 12, 18, 22, 23, 83, 97
Baumann, Gerhard, 155n26
Beethoven, Ludwig van, 11, 23, 69, 86
Besserungsstück, 69, 71
Biedermeier, 11, 70, 71, 76, 78–79, 148
Börne, Ludwig, 18
Brinkmann, Richard, 152n5
Büchner, Georg, 54, 133, 142, 147; *Dantons Tod*, 117
Burgtheater, 11, 14, 15, 19, 27, 69, 73, 75, 76, 128, 129–30, 136, 137
Burkhard, Arthur, 137
Busch, Ernst, 140
Byron, Lord George Gordon, 151n1

Calderón de la Barca, Pedro, 130, 139; *La vido es sueño*, 14, 28
Caroline Augusta, Empress of Austria, 16, 55
censorship, 12, 13, 16, 17, 20, 55, 97
Cermak, Ida, 149n13
Charles V, Holy Roman Emperor, 84
Classicism. *See* French Classicism, German Classicism, Greek Classical ideal
Concordia Society, 18
Crankshaw, Edward, 12

Daffinger, Marie, 23, 25, 61, 81, 82, 88, 89

Daffinger, Moritz, 22, 23, 25, 88
David, Claude, 117
Doblhoff, Anton von, 97
Droste-Hülshoff, Annette von, 148
Dunham, T. C., 45

Ebner-Eschenbach, Marie von, 23
Enlightenment, 80, 130, 140
Expressionism, 54, 118

fate-tragedy, 27–28, 29, 30, 32, 140–41
Feuchtersleben, Ernst von, 148
Francis Joseph, Emperor of Austria, 99, 126
Francis I, Emperor of Austria, 12, 15, 17, 46, 55
Frederick William IV, King of Prussia, 84
French Classicism, 32
Freud, Sigmund, 131
Fricke, Gerhard, 138, 153n35
Fröhlich, Katharina ("Kathi"), 23, 24–25, 81, 83, 86, 94
Fröhlich sisters, 22, 23, 24
Fülleborn, Ulrich, 140

Gasthaus zum Stern, 12, 18
Gasthaus zur Eiche, 23
Geisterstücke, 27
Gellert, Christian, 80
German Classicism and German Classical drama, 32, 33, 34, 39, 40, 53, 127, 130, 131, 132, 133–34, 136, 137, 145
Gesellschaft der Musikfreunde, 86
Goethe, Johann Wolfgang von, 17, 22, 27, 32, 37, 70, 79, 81, 82, 127, 130, 132, 134, 137; *Faust*, 70, 71, 134; *Iphigenie auf Tauris*, 32, 104; *Torquato Tasso*, 32, 35, 37
Gotthelf, Jeremias, 148
Greek Classical ideal, 68
Grillparzer, Adolf (brother), 21